STUDIES IN
ANTHROPOLOGICAL METHOD

General Editors

GEORGE AND LOUISE SPINDLER

Stanford University

STRESS AND
RESPONSE
IN FIELDWORK

STRESS AND
RESPONSE
IN FIELDWORK

Edited by
FRANCES HENRY
McGill University

SATISH SABERWAL
Indian Institute of Advanced Study

HOLT, RINEHART AND WINSTON
New York Chicago San Francisco Atlanta
Dallas Montreal Toronto London Sydney

Copyright © 1969 by Holt, Rinehart and Winston, Inc.
All rights reserved
Library of Congress Catalog Card Number: 72–85343
SBN: 03–077790–9
Printed in the United States of America
1 2 3 4 5 6 7 8 9

FOREWORD

Anthropology has been, since the turn of the century, a significant influence shaping Western thought. It has brought into proper perspective the position of our culture as one of many and has challenged universalistic and absolutistic assumptions and beliefs about the proper condition of man. Anthropology has been able to make this contribution mainly through its descriptive analyses of non-Western ways of life. Only in the last decades of its comparatively short existence as a science have anthropologists developed systematic theories about human behavior in its transcultural dimensions, and only very recently have anthropological techniques of data collection and analysis become explicit and in some instances replicable.

Teachers of anthropology have been handicapped by the lack of clear, authoritative statements of how anthropologists collect and analyze relevant data. The results of fieldwork are available in the ethnographies and they can be used to demonstrate cultural diversity and integration, social control, religious behavior, marriage customs, and the like, but clear, systematic statements about how the facts are gathered and interpreted are rare in the literature readily available to students. Without this information the alert reader of anthropological literature is left uninformed about the process of our science, knowing only of the results. This is an unsatisfying state of affairs for both the student and the instructor.

This series is designed to help solve this problem. Each study in the series focuses upon manageable dimensions of modern anthropological methodology. Each one demonstrates significant aspects of the processes of gathering, ordering, and interpreting data. Some are highly selected dimensions of methodology. Others are concerned with the whole range of experience involved in studying a total society. These studies are written by professional anthropologists who have done fieldwork and have made significant contributions to the science of man and his works. In them the authors explain how they go about this work and to what end. We think they will be helpful to students who want to know what processes of inquiry and ordering stand behind the formal, published results of anthropology.

ABOUT THE AUTHORS

FRANCES HENRY is an associate professor of anthropology at McGill University. She has done extensive research in the Caribbean on religious organization and political development and is currently doing research in Nova Scotia.

SATISH SABERWAL was at McGill University when this volume was edited and is now a Fellow at the Indian Institute of Advanced Study, Simla. He has conducted fieldwork on problems of ethnohistory and culture change among the Embu in Kenya and is currently doing research in India.

PETER C. W. GUTKIND is a professor of anthropology at McGill University. He is interested in urbanization and migration and has conducted extensive fieldwork in East and West Africa.

HANS BUECHLER is an associate professor of Anthropology at Syracuse University. He has conducted research in several areas of Bolivia and Ecuador on problems of land reform and migration.

RONALD WINTROB is a lecturer in the Department of Psychiatry at McGill University. In addition to teaching, research, and clinical practice, he has done research in Liberia.

ABOUT THE BOOK

Stress and Response in Fieldwork is a most timely addition to the series. The relationship of the anthropologist to the people he studies, to the political authorities and power figures of his host community and country, and to himself as observer, participant, and interpreter of behavior have always been matters of deep concern to the profession, though this concern has found written expression less often than one might think. The importance of these matters has been emphasized by the recent changes in access to field situations, in the freedom of inquiry and the uses of social science data created by the transformation of colonies to independent states, and the many ramifications of the cold war. Gaining access to the field, maintaining security for the research, and retaining confidence in the potential contribution of the research results to the benefit of mankind have become more difficult. The increasing difficulties are in part due to political and social barriers created by new and self-conscious governments and to the operation of covert agencies that may use social science data as intelligence data. They are also the concomitant of a growing awareness that the very concept of social science, and especially of anthropology, is a product of the West and the historic relationship of the Western powers with the technologically undeveloped and hitherto politically powerless world populations. These themes run strongly throughout the papers in this symposium. A thoughtful consideration of the problems created by the new milieu of anthropological research should help students to anticipate some of their own problems in the field and the future problems of their discipline.

The ego-centered adjustment of the anthropologist to fieldwork is also a very significant part of the larger complex of problems. For some students the first field experience may serve as a form of therapy. The self-image and social projection of self undergo significant alteration. For others the effects are not so dramatic. In a few cases they may be negative, resulting in loss of self-confidence or the development of suspicious or hostile attitudes toward others. However, for all students of human behavior, fieldwork requires personal adaptation to threatening, if exhilarating, interpersonal situations. The anthropologist as fieldworker is a stranger who, if successful, becomes, if not a friend, at least someone recognized and responded to as part of the social landscape. The anthropologist, however, unlike the immigrant taking up residence in a new community, leaves shortly after having made the adjustment and found acceptance. Anthropologists who have worked in several field situations in depth find themselves accumulating separate social reference systems. Sometimes they even develop more than one social personality. The theme of personal adjustment to the field runs through these papers, sometimes implicitly, often explicitly, and finds culmination in the last chapter, written by a psychiatrist. Again, the student of anthropology can anticipate some of the problems he is likely to encounter in fieldwork by a thoughtful reading of this small volume.

None of the papers of this collection deal with the classical role of the anthropologist in the remote tribal community. This should not be taken as an indication that such experience is unimportant. Many of the themes developed in the present papers, especially those concerning personal social-emotional adaptation, might find particularly full expression in the analysis of such a situation. This role is, and will remain for some time, an ideal model for the anthropologist as fieldworker. However, ideal models, by definition, do not represent reality. The vast majority of the students who will read this booklet will not work in even comparatively unacculturated tribal communities—unless interplanetary exploration unexpectedly makes new tribes available. For anthropologists of the coming generations primitive societies, so recently the forte of the discipline, will be as remote as the societies of the paleolithic men who painted in the caves of Lascaux and Altamira—except for the accounts written by their earlier colleagues. The papers in this volume represent a sample—incomplete to be sure, as it must be—of stress and response in contemporary field situations. They are written by young social scientists of diversified background whose experiences reflect the conditions imposed upon anthropological fieldwork by our times.

GEORGE AND LOUISE SPINDLER

General Editors
Stanford, Calif., May 1969

CONTENTS

STRESS AND
RESPONSE
IN FIELDWORK

Introduction

SATISH SABERWAL and FRANCES HENRY

IELDWORK IS central to the discipline of anthropology. The research strategies and techniques employed have varied, depending in each case upon the researcher's personality, the nature of the sociocultural system studied, and the specific problem for enquiry—if one has been defined before going to the field. In every case, however, the anthropologist has had to face the implications of his role as a stranger, arriving in a community usually unknown previously, intent on establishing extensive information channels rapidly (Nash 1963). This has entailed inevitable difficulties reflected, for example, in Malinowski's diaries (1967) and Evans-Pritchard's famous confrontation with the young Nuer man (1940:12), but we have only recently begun to shed our modesty to discuss the intimate details of our relations with the informants and with the communities we have studied: Bowen (1954), Berreman (1962), Powdermaker (1966), Read (1965), Williams (1967), and the contributors to Casagrande (1960) and to Jongmans and Gutkind (1967) constitute predecessors for the present effort.

Recognizing that the conduct of fieldwork inevitably generates stresses of various sorts, the first four contributors to this volume assess their own responses during fieldwork in diverse circumstances: a Bolivian Amhara community (Buechler), unemployed Nigerian men in Lagos (Gutkind), three different field situations in Trinidad (Henry), and the post-Mau Mau Embu in Kenya (Saberwal). Wintrob contributes a psychiatrist's view of the varied stresses to which the ethnographer is subject in his alien milieu and some of his response patterns in this context.[1] This introduction attempts to summarize their arguments, to highlight their emphases and concerns, and to relate the whole to some of the literature in the field.

---

[1] The diversity in this volume is manifold. Our contributors are from five nations: Canada, England, India, Switzerland, and the United States. Both sexes are represented. Research sponsorship is spread over various North American agencies.

The peasants of Compi studied by Buechler live in self-governing communities with an institutional continuity with their own past. This continuity, manifest despite the profound changes resulting from land reform, invites the ethnographer to look for their social structure in fiestas, community meetings, and other relatively traditional settings whose structure has incorporated new content. Assessing his own and his wife's attempts at establishing rapport with the Compeños, Buechler analyzes the manner in which the ethnographer's status in this community is "assimilated" into that of his interpreter; the interpreter's communication channels in some measure define the ethnographer's. Social, political, and economic ties between migrants and their home community provided Buechler with further channels for inquiry in the city of La Paz, where many Compeños go in search of work.

Though Saberwal's interpreters rank much lower in their community than Buechler's, they do provide access to settings where he is not invited; thus he learns about the political party's nominating procedures from an interpreter who is a candidate for nomination. In addition, he tells us that the community probably used the interpreters for information to make *its own assessment* of the ethnographer. Here we are reminded of Berreman's report (1962) from a highly stratified society: The interpreter's status determines the ethnographer's communication channels. High-caste informants feel comfortable with a high-caste Hindu interpreter but not with a Muslim; the reverse is the case with the low-caste informants.[2]

Agrarian reform and migration have produced orderly change in Buechler's community. The Mau Mau uprising, a bloody insurrection in Kenya, was much more disruptive of the Embu social order, and its memory was an important determinant of Embu relationships with each other and with outsiders, including the ethnographer. Saberwal describes a series of situations of varying measures of awkwardness, and his efforts at maintaining his relationships in good repair. It is in the political party, however, that he faced the most determined opposition, reflecting the suspicion and hostility continuing from the Mau Mau days. The intensity of feelings was such that he chose to withdraw from further enquiry into the contemporary political process. To press or not to press: The necessary feel for judgment comes only through disciplined observation of the pattern of the others' responses to one's own actions.

Examining the nature of the Embu society elsewhere, Saberwal (1969) shows that the contemporary Embu cannot be understood without the use of wider perspectives in time and space; attention to contemporary decision-making centers, at least at the national level, is vital. This theme of the inadequacy of ahistorical analyses of isolates finds expression in the papers of both Henry and Gutkind as well.

Aware of the intimate and extensive interaction between the political elite and the masses in the island of Trinidad, Frances Henry seeks to understand the political process in unorthodox ways. Following a study of the Shango cult,

---

[2] Béteille (1965), working without an interpreter, established close relations with the Brahmins in a south Indian village; this entailed that his contacts with the lowest castes be brief and furtive.

she returned to her familar island and used surveys to probe the nature of the political commitment among the voters, and intensive interviews to determine political orientations in the Trinidadian elite. In the context of her own inquiries, she gives a fieldworker's-eye view of the hazards of governmental scrutiny, of picking a sample, of training the interviewers, and of doing research in the halls of power. Anthropologists are new to this domain of inquiry, and Henry's interests shade gently into those of the political scientists.

This resistance to the lowering of disciplinary barriers is manifest in Gutkind's reflections too. As he gets to know the unemployed men of Lagos, he is impressed with the "multiplexity" of his observations: The social organization of the unemployed was "rooted in far more complex matters of macroeconomic and political change, and . . . many aspects of modernization and national development would have to be considered." Finding that the familiar research procedures may not fit the research situation inevitably creates stress for the fieldworker. The stress is manifold, however, and Gutkind's paper encapsulates its varieties.

There is, first, the *primary stress of involvement* which confronts the fieldworker seeking to establish rapport with strangers: Between them is a situation of complementarity, with the fieldworker wishing to learn and to get the data, and the people among whom he works having the capacity—and sometimes the wish—to teach and to provide the data. Gutkind examines his own shock and bewilderment during the first encounter with the "universe" of his research. Often the fieldworker seeks to convert the situation into a relationship of participation and reciprocity; this is illustrated in the papers of Buechler and Saberwal. The beginner in his first field experience, or an old hand entering unfamiliar territory, often feels threatened by the uncertainties of the situation. Wintrob analyzes some characteristic responses with the psychiatrist's concepts—and sensitivity—and we can do no better than ask the reader to turn to Wintrob's contribution, a paper without precedent in our discipline.

Second, both Gutkind and Wintrob invite our attention to what might be called the *secondary stress of commitment.* They suggest that one's relations with the people studied lead to an intense involvement with "my people," "my tribe," or "the people of my village." This may not be quite as patronizing as some nonprofessionals believe, but Wintrob provides cases to illustrate Gutkind's view that it may produce conflicts in the performance of one's professional tasks. While the anthropologist-host community relationship spans the entire range from copious-tears-at-parting to mutual detestation, we may suggest, following Roe (1952) and Nash (1963), that an anthropologist is likely to be productive if he has developed enough of an "autonomous personality" to be able to keep his affects and his cognitions separate.

Third, an anthropologist going into the field often finds his *research design under stress.* Given the diversity of the peoples of the world, the range of anthropological interests, and the small number of anthropologists, one rarely has information about a society adequate for preparing a reliable research design before going to the field; more often, research designs prepared with loving care five- or ten-thousand miles away turn out to have no relevance to the contemporary scene. Needless to say, the situation can generate acute anxieties concerning one's changing role identity in relation to one's professional career; Wintrob, Gutkind, and Henry discuss the issues at some length.

Finally, there is a cluster of factors which can be designated the *stress of politicization*, difficult to escape in the 1960s. In moving from the certainties of the colonial period to new indigenous equilibriums, societies round the world are engaged in important political changes. Henry and Saberwal choose deliberately to focus on these processes, but Gutkind, whose primary concern is elsewhere, also has to attend to the politics of his society. Politics are about power, and however fascinating its workings, those who have it are best approached with care, especially if a precarious and uncertain hold makes them nervous. Where the administrative structure is weak, with weakly established rules subject to unpredictable interpretation, the researcher's level of anxiety can often rise abruptly. Excitable dispositions are unhelpful in such events.

It is also true, however, as Saberwal points out, that social science results have been used by the government of the United States (and, indeed, some other governments) for purposes anthropologists may not approve of or even know about. The anthropologist, "the man in the middle," and his discipline anthropology thus come under extraordinary stress, emanating from the shifting content of international political attitudes and relations, especially as these pertain to field research.[3] During his fieldwork the ethnographer, seeking relations of reciprocity with his community, is necessarily solicitous of its welfare. Furthermore, it is only human for him to foster the impression that his inquiries will contribute to its future welfare too; but, in fact, however marginal to his own society, the ethnographer's primary commitments, his primary expectations in life, are integral to the affluent West—the third world does not count. It is easy for him to begin to judge his own interest in the non-Western world in adverse terms. Saberwal concludes his paper with a query as to his own trustworthiness; many other anthropologists find their situations equally distressing.

One of the elements in this impasse is the fact that overwhelming numbers of anthropologists come from North America and western Europe, define their problems in terms more relevant to the state of their discipline in their home countries than to any concerns of the host country, and publish their work in their home country. One way of escaping this is by working through institutions in the host country, on problems defined in its context, training local research workers, and so forth. This method can, of course, generate its own stresses, and Henry discusses briefly the problems of research design and the use of local interviewers.

In sum, then, five young social scientists present here their view of their own field experience during the 1960s. We are passing through a period of historic importance for anthropology. International research on the scale we have witnessed in recent years is something new for the human family. If it turns out that the financial support for this research has been politically motivated, or if the peoples who are the frequent subjects of research decide on their own that this is so, the recent bounty is likely to end abruptly. We have no prescience of the course history

---

[3] These shifts have in recent years been expressed sharply: The host country may deny permission for research or, having given it, withdraw it and expel the researcher in short order.

will take, but in the hope that fieldwork will continue along honorable lines, beneficial to all who make it possible, we would like to conclude with three comments.

First, as Buechler points out, retrospective analysis of one's own field relations improves one's understanding of the manner in which one's research developed; it is important that fieldworkers should include in their notes detailed records concerning their relationships with their informants. How a society receives and relates to the "stranger" says much about its values; it is worthy of disciplined attention.

Second, Wintrob's concluding query is intriguing:

> If it is true that psychological stress reactions are as common and as important to the performance and reporting of field research as this report would suggest, then what practical means could be utilized to extend the fieldworker's understanding of his own psychological needs and responses, and to broaden his understanding of the psychological significance of the reactions of the people he sets out to study?

In a way the present volume, and the others we mentioned at the beginning, belong to the "practical means" needed for the purpose; here and there it may also be possible to develop courses in research methods which enable a psychiatrist to convey his insights into the handling of stress to students in anthropology.

Third, the essays which follow have tended to emphasize the element of stress in fieldwork. A volume could be produced, with equal ease, focusing on the pleasures of fieldwork. Establishing warm, personal relationships with members of the host society—informants, interpreters, assistants, friends—is one of the most gratifying experiences open to an anthropologist.

1

The Social Position
of an Ethnographer
in the Field[1]

HANS C. BUECHLER

I T IS DIFFICULT if not impossible for an ethnographer to make a rigorously scientific assessment of his position within the social organization of an alien society. It may be argued that only another investigator, preferably one from a culture different from that of the ethnographer, would be sufficiently removed from the situation to successfully accomplish this task. However, such an experiment would be difficult to undertake. I have yet to meet an anthropologist who would be willing to submit to such a test. Nevertheless, an assessment of his position in the field is of utmost importance for any anthropologist, both in measuring his effectiveness as a researcher and as a tool for interpreting social relations themselves. At some time or other, probably every anthropologist is compelled to analyze his place in the society he studies because his position determines to a large extent what channels of information are open to him. The channels of information in turn are a crucial factor in defining the information itself. Therefore, if an anthropologist examines his social position in the field for heuristic purposes rather than for formal analysis, such a venture would appear to be legitimate. It is in this sense that this chapter is conceived. I do not pretend that my analysis of my position vis-à-vis my informants is strictly scientific. I merely hope to provide some insight into the means by which an anthropologist elicits response, the difficulties he incurs in his task, and the ways in which this approach may give him valuable clues about the society itself.

[1] Research on which this chapter is based was supported by a Columbia Traveling Fellowship, by the Bolivia project of the Research Institute for the Study of Man, by Peace Corps Grant 397, and by the Canada Council. Thanks also go to my wife Judith-Maria Buechler for editorial help in writing this paper and for permitting me to use examples from her own experience.

This chapter will focus on two field trips to Bolivia. During the first trip I spent sixteen months working with peasants from Compi, a Titicaca lake-shore community, and with migrants from the same community to La Paz, Bolivia's government seat. On the second trip, which had a duration of three months, I concentrated on feasts and migrant organizations in La Paz. I shall analyze my position with respect to Compi villagers and migrants in the following manner. First, I shall present some details of my own background which may shed some light on the subject. This will be followed by a short description of Compi. Then I shall examine the ways in which contacts were established and how these contacts affected my social position in Compi. Beginning with the preliminary contact in the community and with the choice of an interpreter, I shall describe the persons involved in these contacts as intermediaries between the community and myself. Next I shall study the means by which I was able to penetrate personally into the mainstream of Compi life by participating actively in some important activities. Finally, I shall analyze the ways in which the position I succeeded in establishing was endangered and how my contacts with Compi residents and migrants facilitated the study of La Paz feasts and migrant organizations. At every step I shall compare my own experience with that of my wife. She was studying child-rearing patterns and market relations. Her position in the community differed from my own because her informants were primarily women and children, while mine were for the most part men. This provides a comparison of male and female channels of communication. In conclusion I present the importance of this method.

I

I was not a complete stranger to Bolivian culture when I conducted my first fieldwork there. Born of Swiss parents, I grew up in La Paz, Bolivia, went to a Bolivian school until the fifth grade, and spent most of my vacations in a peasant community near Compi. So I was familiar with the Bolivian national culture in which Aymara migrants participate to a large extent. I had also had some contact with Aymara peasant culture. However, I was always looked upon as a foreigner by Bolivians and accepted this role myself.

My first field experience came in 1961 when I was working as a field assistant to an American anthropologist in an Aymara community. In the summer of 1963 I carried out a survey of former landed estates which had been expropriated and divided among the peasants by the agrarian reform of 1953. In November 1964 I returned to one of the former estates visited during the survey for an intensive study on land reform and migration. Finally, in the summer of 1967 I concentrated on fiestas and migrant groups in La Paz.

Before analyzing my social position in Compi I shall present a brief sketch of the community. Compi is a small, dispersed agricultural community of 1230 inhabitants situated on the Panamerican Highway, some fifty miles northwest of the city of La Paz. Previous to 1953 it was a large landholding, or hacienda, where each peasant family provided the owner with twelve man-labor days per week plus other services in return for the use of one to four acres of land. After the promulgation of the land reform decree of 1953 most of the land was turned over to the former hacienda peasants. The land which the former owner had been allowed to retain was also purchased bit by bit by individual peasants.

Compi peasants do not form a single cohesive unit. The community is divided into five sections, each with its own government, which act independently in most matters. Only education and larger fiestas are matters concerning the entire community. Sectional leadership positions are held in rotation. They include the secretary-general, who acts as chairman at assemblies and as section representative in feasts and matters concerning the whole community, the *jilakata*, who replaces him in his absence and who is in charge of agricultural ritual, a sectional representative to the community school, and the like. The criteria for section leadership and prestige in general are married status, age, official positions held previously, and the number of feasts sponsored by an individual. Bachelors may attend assemblies but do not voice their opinions. Similarly, the opinions of those who have not sponsored village feasts and who have not yet held official positions generally do not carry much weight. However, in recent years knowledge of Spanish and personal connections with officials in the capital have gained in importance as criteria for leadership. Especially in the years immediately following the agrarian reform, one's ability to "pull strings" in the La Paz bureaucracy was important in accelerating land expropriation. Therefore, young Spanish speakers were often preferred to older unilingual Aymara speakers for leadership positions. Bilingual persons continue to retain essential functions, a fact which proves crucial in establishing rapport. However, at present section heads are nominated according to the old prestige system again. The addition of a new criterion to the prestige system therefore did not reduce the weight of the traditional one permanently. Fiestas, for instance are as important as ever. Every man is expected to undertake a number of *cargos*, or sponsorships, during his lifetime. Shortly before or after marriage, a man (and in Compi even some unwed women) organizes a dance group for Carnival. He asks his peers to dance in his group and hires a band (either with his own money or with contributions collected from the dancers), and is always the first to serve alcohol during the feast. In his lifetime, he assumes progressively more onerous *cargos* until he has exhausted most of the possibilities open to him. Only then is he considered an elder whose opinion in community affairs is honored fully. The status achieved by a person through sponsorship of fiestas is recognized by all the sections. The entire community participates in the major feasts, but they are organized on a sectional basis. Fiestas, therefore, simultaneously reflect the unity of the community and its fragmentation into sections.

A final criterion of leadership is magic. Each section has one or more magicians who officiate in public fertility rituals whose purpose it is to attract rain, to disperse hailstorms, or to assure a good harvest. The voice of the magicians therefore does not remain unheeded in section assemblies.

In spite of the importance of section and community activities, most of Compi life revolves around the family and kinsmen. Even community life is determined to a large extent by kinship ties. Most of the persons who aid a Compeño in sponsoring a feast are relatives. Moreover, marriage creates the main links between sections and between Compi and Llamacachi. Kinship also regulates inheritance of land and to a large extent defines the group of people with whom one interacts most frequently. Kin ties have also become avenues for contact with the city. Many Compeños migrated to La Paz as a result of harsh conditions on the hacienda and later as a result of land pressure. Family ties with these migrants have become an integral part of marketing onions, Compi's cash crop. Onions are usually sold by the producer himself. Migrants provide lodgings for their relatives from the country and those migrants who sell on the markets themselves are instrumental in disposing of the produce their country kin were not able to sell. Conversely, migrants frequently continue to have access to land in their home community. Some even reestablish themselves in Compi after having lived in La Paz for some time. These contacts between the Compeños and persons whose way of life had been considerably changed by the city contributed in defining my role in the field.

In spite of the villagers' contacts with returned migrants and their own experiences in La Paz, they do not have a generally open attitude toward strangers. Like most Aymara, Compeños remain quite reserved even toward members of neighboring communities. This attitude is instilled in them from childhood. Preschool-age children usually hide when a stranger approaches the house. Even Aymara folktales warn against socializing with strangers: A lover, whose background is unknown may turn out to be a snake, a lizard, or a skunk in human disguise. A Compeño may have a handful of friends or acquaintances in other communities, but most contacts are confined to the community. Thus, an outsider must first prove his good intentions before he becomes generally accepted, and even after his acceptance his status is never taken entirely for granted.

II

I first visited Compi in the summer of 1963, when I was conducting a survey of former haciendas. I discovered that the simplest way to obtain information quickly was to interview the secretaries-general. Therefore, I called on Rufino, the secretary-general of one of the sections of Compi. I was directed to his house by Severo, a teen-ager who spoke very little Spanish but was eager to help me. Rufino immediately showed me the legal titles to his plots, probably convinced, in spite of my denial, that I was an official from the National Council for Agrarian Reform. His son, on the other hand, provided me with the information I wanted. He spoke some Spanish and had been to La Paz frequently. Intrigued by the complex community structure of this ex-hacienda, I decided to return to Compi for prolonged fieldwork in November 1964. Prevailing on the contact with Severo I had established the year before, I visited the secretaries-general of all the sections with him as interpreter and guide. Although everyone said that the matter would have to be discussed in a section meeting, all except for one seemed positive about my study. The secretary-general who did not favor my study would probably also have approved had we not been joined by an older influential man who spoke strongly against it. I hoped, however, that there would be enough persons in my favor once the section meeting was held. This hope proved to be illusory. I found out soon enough that even if only one or two elders persistently oppose a proposal in an assembly, this can be sufficient to force the assembly to drop the matter or to postpone its discussion to some future meeting when that person is absent. In effect, when I happened to chance upon a meeting held a few days later, two persons' dissent was sufficient to bar me from the section, at least officially.

In the meantime, however, I had also established contact with other persons. Severo insisted that I meet Paz, whom he considered the real leader of the community. Paz turned out to be a returned migrant who had lived in the cities of La Paz and Cochabamba for a number of years. When I was introduced to him, he was planting cherry trees (which are practically unknown on the altiplano) oeside a pool he had made himself and which he intended to stock with fish from Cochabamba. He wore a Cochabamba-type straw hat and a strikingly patterned pullover sweater which he had knitted himself. He spoke excellent Spanish without any ·Aymara accent. Paz expressed strong interest in the study and promised me that his "brother" Pedro (actually a distant relative) would help to introduce me to the community. Such an opportunity presented itself a few days later at a festival to celebrate the end of the school year, which was attended by the school authorities of every section and by some other community officials. With Paz at his side Pedro translated my research plans into Aymara, urging all present to support me. A few persons nodded their heads in approval. One or two others commented that they had seen me in a fiesta in nearby Tiquina playing the panpipes with a group of peasants. I was therefore not a complete stranger, an important fact, especially for the more traditional elements in the community. Only one younger man suggested that section meetings be called first before reaching a decision. On this occasion Aymara decision-making seemed to run in my favor for Pedro replied quickly that recourse to section meetings was unnecessary. Since the young man did not pursue the matter any further, my immediate acceptance was considered approved. Later I discovered that Pedro was the community's principal school authority in charge of coordinating school construction and maintenance. He had lived in La Paz for a long time, had married a Pazeña, and had recently settled in the community. He was one of the few politically active persons in the area. In fact he continued to travel frequently to La Paz in connection with his function as party campaigner. The contacts he had established in La Paz became useful as means of obtaining financial support for community projects. Thanks to his unique capacities as a returned migrant, Pedro was held in high esteem by Compeños. He was accepted in the circle of the elders in spite of the fact that he was young and had not sponsored a single fiesta. I discovered later that he, Paz, and a few other returned migrants handled most matters concerning officials and visitors from La Paz. My case was therefore within his sphere of influence. He and Paz were interested in my coming in order to establish further links with the outside world. Even though I had no technical assistance to offer, it was possible that my "connections" (whatever their nature might be) could benefit the community and perhaps even themselves. In the case of Paz, there was also the desire to share experience acquired outside the somewhat restricting world of Compi.

I did not consider the approval of the school authorities a sufficient entrée into the community. From previous experience I knew that decisions on most matters were made in meetings where the secretary-general and a good proportion of the family heads were present. Since there were no community meetings apart from school authority meetings, I attended sectional ones. This was important since Pedro, in spite of his prestige, could not represent the elders in the community fully. Without the all-out support of the elders I risked remaining marginal to the mainstream of community life.

For a month I worked without an Aymara interpreter, using only inform- ants who spoke Spanish. Then I decided to employ Paz. He was one of the few persons who could read and write as well as speak Spanish fluently. He was not only respected by the community but he also seemed genuinely interested in my work. He had enjoyed a position of authority for many years and had acquired enough prestige to sit with the elders, although he had sponsored only minor fiestas. As I have already mentioned, he acted as a "culture broker" with officials and institutions in the capital. As a result, he was able to provide entrée into the powerful circles in the community. Moreover, he was always well informed about important happenings concerning the community as a whole and his section in particular. Working with a person specifically associated with one section had some drawbacks, however; it became increasingly difficult not to be associated with Paz' section of the community alone and to be left out of events in the other sec- tions. For instance, Paz always knew when there would be a meeting in his own section, but I missed many a meeting in other sections because I did not hear about it in time. My identification with Paz' section was most apparent during the large fiestas in which the entire community participated. I was expected to sit with the elders of Paz' section and, as we shall see later, I danced only in "my" section.

My identification with a particular section did not prevent me from estab- lishing numerous contacts in other sections. Apart from connections I had established before I hired Paz, some channels were opened through Paz himself. Since the endogamic unit[1] is the community and not the section a person has rela- tives in a number of sections. Paz had close relatives in all sections but one and also in Llamacachi, a neighboring community. Most of these relatives became good informants. Paz' kinship ties even gave me access to informants in Cawaya, a section where my study had been officially rejected. Furthermore, Paz knew many of the younger men because they had played soccer together. The fact that I was invited to sit with the elders during sectional fiestas of any of the sections to which I had official access reflects these connections.

Paz' family ties also permitted me to gather good family histories and minute data on family structure. The closer the relatives, the more intimate the details that became known to me. Through the use of an interpreter I was thus placed in a particular position with respect to the community. I was, in a sense, assimilated with his place in Compi social organization. To a certain extent obli- gations to Paz were due to me also and vice versa. The consequences of the use of an interpreter, therefore, were more extensive than the mere surmounting of language barriers.

The importance of channels of communication opened through interpreters became even more apparent to me when my wife, herself an anthropologist, joined

---

[1] The group of persons from which a Compeño may select a spouse.

me in the field after our marriage seven months after the beginning of fieldwork. She took an interpreter from Llamacachi and in so doing expanded comprehension of that community.

My wife was also able to gain access to significant channels of communication in another way. As a man I had not been able to talk to many women; in fact the female view of society was practically closed to me, for except for relatives, Aymara men do not interact with women frequently. The fact that I was known in the community greatly facilitated my wife's acceptance. Moreover, the fact that she was herself doing anthropological work probably did not surprise anyone since Compi women, in addition to working in their households or in their fields, also work independently by selling onions in La Paz. However, gaining rapport with the women was far from automatic. Women attend community meetings only when the male household head is absent, and it is imperative for the household to be represented at the meeting, or when a complaint is lodged against them; and they do not hold separate meetings. Therefore, it was impossible for my wife to explain the nature of her study to the women as a group. So she had to rely initially on the already established relationships between her informants' husbands and me. The second difficulty arose from the fact that few women were qualified to act as interpreters. The two mestizo women in the community seemed too marginal to the mainstream of Compi life to be considered. Furthermore, mestizo prejudice toward Aymara peasants was apt to harm the study. However, most of the women who had migrated to La Paz and as a result had some knowledge of Spanish were either not fluent enough or were married. It is not surprising that our first choice of an interpreter turned out to be disastrous. We hired a nineteen-year-old sister of one of my best Llamacachi informants who had worked in La Paz as a market vendor. We found very soon that her Spanish left much to be desired. The fact that my wife did not speak fluent Spanish at the beginning of fieldwork compounded this problem. Furthermore, this girl had lost most of her connections with her home community. Worst of all, however, she was embarrassed to ask many of the questions which my wife asked her to translate, such as questions regarding conception. This embarrassment awoke the suspicion of some of her informants. We soon found that informal means of communicating information through relatives and school children were an effective substitute for the lack of formal means. Nasty rumors circulated about my wife's study, with the effect that one potential informant even ran away when she saw my wife approaching. After a week of suffering we ended the experiment by giving the interpreter leave, much to her own relief, for she had actively tried to bring about her dismissal.

My wife met Sofia, her second interpreter, during a community feast, where Sofia interpreted conversations and prayers for her without even having been asked to do so. Sofia was a nineteen-year-old girl from Llamacachi. She had grown up in La Paz and had been educated there. Later she had returned to Llamacachi with her mother, who had found that business was better there than in La Paz. Since Sofia was very outgoing, she was soon accepted as a member of the community and, because of her experience in La Paz, was frequently consulted by Llamacachi girls on subjects ranging from marriage to fiesta clothes. Her mother's store, which she helped manage, became an "information center" where all the community gossip was aired. So Sofia's role resembled that of the official male "culture brokers." She acted as an assistant to the priest who says Mass and a dentist who treated patients once a week in the neighboring community. In view of this position it was not surprising that she should have sought to establish contact with my wife. Sofia turned out to be an excellent interpreter. Through her "information center" most members of Llamacachi learned what the study was all about. Thus Llama-cachi informants were already personally prepared before my wife interviewed them. As in the case of Paz, however, relatives and kin became the main informants. Through Sofia I also began to understand the concerns of her community.

III

Dissociating myself from certain preconceived roles usually ascribed to strangers and placing myself in positions with respect to the social organization of the villagers which would permit access to information through the intermediary of certain community members was but the first step in gaining rapport. A criterion which may have been even more important was my willingness and ability to participate in community life. From previous experience I knew that it was important never to refuse food or alcohol when it was offered. In Compi only Protestants do not drink and even they are usually forced to do so on occasion. Abstinence is considered a refusal to maintain social relations with the host and as a result Protestants are not only in an awkward and marginal position during fiestas but frequently even abstain from attending community meetings. My full participation in fiestas ranging from the ceremony that accompanies a child's first haircut to funerals and saint's day's celebrations further enhanced rapport. However, my contribution to community life did not necessarily have to be orthodox. Frequently I was called upon to perform tasks which only I could carry out since my potential as a foreigner could be combined with my ability to imitate Aymara customs. Thus, during fiestas I not only sat with the elders drinking and chewing coca but served as a chauffeur to transport a bridal pair to a wedding or a sponsor from his home to the location of a fiesta. I could also be called upon to drive sick persons to a nearby mission clinic, and I rarely traveled alone to La Paz. I also served as a photographer. Similarly, my wife was granted considerable flexibility with respect to etiquette and custom in general. During fiestas women are supposed to accompany their husbands and sit on the ground apart from the men. Although my wife did accompany me to fiestas, she did not do so invariably. On one occasion she was asked who would lead me home when I became intoxicated. She answered that I had to write down my observations while at the fiesta and drive the car home afterwards; therefore, I would not drink too much. This explanation was accepted.

My best connections, however, came through my interest in Aymara music. The emancipation of the peasant brought about by the agrarian reform awoke national interest in folklore. Groups of Aymara and Quechua musicians are frequently invited to play traditional instruments in La Paz and elsewhere. This in turn has resulted in a kind of renaissance of music played with traditional instruments in the peasant communities themselves. Many of the instruments had fallen into disuse as they were replaced by brass bands, but now old instruments were being unearthed once more, and new ones were ordered from artisans in a distant community. Since I had learned how to play the panpipes, I was invited to perform with a group of players from my interpreter's section who planned to play at a festival in La Paz. My recordings of the music were brought to a radio station on the high plateau for broadcasting. Since almost every peasant home has a transistor radio, the prestige of coming on the air was considerable. In fact, since the inception of the Aymara music program, dozens of ensembles arrived at the radio station to have their music recorded. Although the group with whom I performed finally did not go to the festival, I was soon flooded with requests to record music of most of the community's sections and later of sections of other communities. Thus I was able to make an almost complete collection of traditional and new music played in the area with ideal conditions. At this time, an educated migrant to La Paz working for the tourist bureau decided to organize a folklore festival in Compi itself. Dance groups from the entire area were invited to participate. Tourists and high government officials arrived by carfuls and busloads. Since that time, the festival has been held annually, attracting increasingly larger crowds. The success of the festival also induced two sections of the community to reintroduce panpipes which had not been in use for over a decade in one of their minor feasts. I was invited to participate in this feast, this time to head a dance group. Thus I gained information on the preparation of fiestas, the obligations of each participant, and the meaning of ritual, which would have been extremely difficult to obtain otherwise.

For instance, my participation in ritual turned my attention to the adaptation of rules of ritual and etiquette to different situations. During everyday interaction I was not expected to conform to all Aymara forms of politeness. It was sufficient if I observed the most obvious ones such as never failing to greet a person even if I had met him only a short time before. It was also easy to avoid breaches of etiquette by imitating the behavior of my interpreter. However, as a participant in a fiesta, where failure to conform to etiquette and ritual frequently results in drunken brawls, it would have been considered an affront if I had not at least tried to abide by the rules of the game as best as I could. In my position as a dance group leader I was supposed to act as a representative of "my" section just like all the other dancers. I was no longer considered a stranger.

Descriptions of ritual sometimes strike one as improbable because they only take their ideal or official form into consideration. Trying to follow ritual rules personally made it possible for me to understand what conforming to them really entailed. It led me to analyze roles such as that of older persons who accompany and advise fiesta sponsors. I began to understand which rules were obligatory and which ones could be altered or circumvented, as well as how this could be accomplished. Since a community member's prestige, on the one hand, and harmony in the community, on the other, depend to a large extent on his ability to interpret the applicability and the margins of liberty of ritual rules in any given situation, the actual *practice* of ritual is probably as important, if indeed not more so, than the rituals themselves.

I became a part of such calculations of priorities and of the margin of liberty of ritual rules myself when I participated in the dance group of my interpreter's section. The fact that I had been chosen by the sponsor of the dance group to lead the dancers was in itself significant in this respect. The sponsor was generally considered to be tight-fisted. This conclusion had been arrived at because he was often seen drinking at home accompanied by his wife, a thing unheard of in a society where drinking is a social act par excellence. It was rumored that he had decided to sponsor the feast only because he could expect a number of persons whom he had helped sponsor fiestas to reciprocate on this occasion. As a person who was not completely integrated into the community, I could be expected to demand little alcohol and food for the dancers, a function incumbent upon the dance group leader. Actually the rumors about the sponsor's motives achieved some credibility when, on the last day of the feast, the dancers were offered less than the customary gift of meat, bread, and fruit which must be provided as a token of gratitude for having participated in the dance group. The second dance leader was indignant enough to refuse the gift in spite of repeated prodding on the part of the sponsor to accept it.

In spite of my rather special place in this fiesta, my image was enhanced. As we shall see later, my ability to play the panpipes aided me in re-establishing cordial relations after I had temporarily lost much of the villagers' sympathy due to unfortunate circumstances.

Maintaining rapport in Compi was not accomplished without setbacks. Once I felt obliged to discharge two persons whom I had hired to take a census of the community. Since one of the persons held an important position in the community, he tried for a time to have me expelled. This was unsuccessful since Aymara peasants dislike an open showdown except when under the influence of alcohol. Moreover, it is against Aymara custom to take sides openly in a quarrel which is of no direct concern to oneself. A meeting was called to discuss the matter, but few persons appeared and I was not informed when it took place. I was finally able to explain my reasons for dismissing my assistants to the secretary-general of the section concerned; after that work continued normally.

Another difficult situation was created through circumstances beyond our control. In the middle of fieldwork we were joined by a medical student with no previous fieldwork experience. Since he was interested in native pharmacopoeia, my wife asked her assistant to draw up a list of persons who were knowledgeable in this matter. She accomplished this with the help of her mother, who is a curer herself. Although the student was warned not to show the list to his informants, he did not heed my wife's advice. The resulting uproar could have terminated our research in Llamacachi. It turned out that most of the curers were also magicians. There is considerable ambivalence about magicians among the Aymara because every magician is also a potential sorcerer. The practice of sorcery is kept secret even among the magicians themselves. So the list could be interpreted as a possible means of investigating sorcery, which is considered an extremely serious offense.

The rumor soon spread that the medical student would take the names of the magicians to the United States from whence orders would be issued to arrest and punish them. This rumor worried my wife's interpreter because someone had recognized her handwriting, and her mother, of course, was distraught. The medical student was forced to accelerate his study in Llamacachi, terminating it in the next three days before public opinion became too negative. Fortunately my wife was not suspected. A few days later she was able to explain the matter to the most important magician in the community, whose family had always been very friendly to her. He accepted her explanation that she had had the list drawn up because of the project's interest in gathering medical lore, and so the problem was clarified and considered closed.

IV

Serious difficulties which did affect my fieldwork arose when I returned to Compi for a month in the summer of 1967 to complete my material on fiestas. Paradoxically, I was greeted as a long-lost friend by the very elders of the section who had previously barred my study. As a matter of fact, when I attended a fiesta there, I was honored as an elder of the community, the highest compliment that could be bestowed upon me. However, an alarming number of persons from the section I knew best refused to talk to me. I discovered that all the community members interviewed in a follow-up survey conducted by the project I had been associated with had received cash payments for their contribution. I personally kept to the policy of remunerating only those persons who worked for me full-time. I was convinced that indiscriminate awards would be considered as bribes and would create jealousy among them. Others expected me to pay them this time. Worst of all, however, some persons seemed to feel that they could not talk to me because they might be accused of "selling information" to me. At the end of the month I returned to La Paz (where I planned to study fiestas and migrant groups) somewhat disillusioned and a bit hurt. Even though there were always persons who would talk to me, the prospect of being snubbed by Compeños with whom I formerly had enjoyed excellent rapport lowered my morale. In fact, I often preferred to work with my interpreter's close kin, who had not changed their attitude toward me.

I returned to Compi only three times in the subsequent three months that I worked in La Paz. This was sufficient, however, to mend the strained relationship. Things began to improve when I was asked to dance in the annual folklore festival in Compi. I declined the invitation since I was not able to attend the practice sessions, but I did play the panpipes with a dance group after the main presentation. When I returned to Compi a few days later for a special rite which took place in the middle of the night, the persons who took part in it, including a young man who had avoided me a few weeks earlier, were as cordial to me as they had ever been. Two months later I was asked to dance again with the Compeños, this time in a festival in La Paz. A day after the festival I invited some of the dancers to play at my brother's wedding. Thus I had attained a position in the community which was not very different from that of a Compi migrant to La Paz. This position was invaluable for my study in La Paz. Since I had only three months to do fieldwork there, I needed channels which would permit me to gain the confidence of informants rapidly. This was especially important for my study on fiestas where participants scatter in no time after the event and therefore are difficult to interview once the fiesta is over. Since Compeño migrants live dispersed over many neighborhoods of La Paz, it was not rare for one or more of them to be dancing in any given neighborhood fiesta. Where this was the case, I had easy access to information both by interviewing these migrants themselves and by having them introduce me to the organizers of dance groups. Much of my most detailed information was gathered in this way. My wife, who was studying market women, profited considerably from migrant channels as well, all the more so since her assistant, the same one she had had in Llamacachi, was herself a part-time market vendor and minor union leader.

The importance of our Compi contacts with respect to our work in La Paz can best be appreciated when contrasted with other means of gathering information which we tried. Generally contact with complete strangers seemed somewhat simpler when they were approached through our assistants, despite their embarrassment at talking to strangers. However, these interviews rarely had much depth. Interviewing the same persons repeatedly and slowly gaining rapport in this way was impractical because of the short duration of the study and because of their erratic schedules. Moreover, informants have vague addresses which made it difficult to locate them. The only other means of establishing new fruitful contacts was by attending meetings of market unions. However, close individual ties with union members would have taken longer to establish than the three months which were available to us.

Conclusions

The kinds of information an anthropologist is able to gather in the field depend on his access to channels of information. These in turn depend on the command he has over persons who are in strategic positions within the social organization of the group studied and who are thus in the nexus of the communication network. In order to attain this command, the anthropologist must establish multiple relationships within the group. He may establish these through informal and formal contacts with persons representing different institutions and by his own participation in the activities of the group. The relationships which he has been able to establish in this manner define his position within the social organization of the group.

Therefore, by retracing the steps he has taken to establish his social position, an anthropologist can assess the directions his research has taken, locate possible overemphasis or underemphasis of his data, and even attempt to define the social system itself. This in turn can help him supplement his research by adding new channels of information.

The utility of this procedure becomes apparent when one attempts to predict the ways in which the research situation could have developed if other alternatives in establishing rapport had been adopted. Had I introduced myself into the community through the teachers, I would probably not have gotten very far since most of them are strangers with few ties with community members. Had I employed Pedro instead of Paz as an interpreter, my insight into sectional divisions might have been reduced but I might have attained deeper understanding of the life of migrants, not only because Pedro himself continued to travel to La Paz constantly but also because his wife was born in the city. Finally, had I not actively participated in fiestas, rapport might not have been re-established at the end of my second visit to Compi.

To be sure, channels of communication can often be tapped through mere trial and error. However, insight into the mechanisms involved enable the researcher to provide more direction to his efforts. Moreover, the analysis of the progression of his field research may in itself become a part of his collected data. In this way method and results become more closely aligned as integrated parts of ethnography.

2

The Social Researcher
in the Context of
African National Development:
Reflections on an Encounter

PETER C. W. GUTKIND

A few years back the European anthropologist may have been able on the
West Coast [of Africa] to glean some information about customs and beliefs;
at all events he had as good a chance of doing so as in any other region of the
world. Nowadays the African has a very shrewd idea of what the anthropologist
would like him to say; and the information is in consequence becoming less and
less authentic. The African's power of self-organization is manifesting itself partly
in political movements of one kind and another, and partly in his increasing
facility of keeping the European guessing. (Le Gros Clark 1953:153–54)

I

I think it is fair to suggest that most anthropologists believe it is possible
to do fieldwork anywhere, providing that they have been trained in methodological skills and show a ready understanding of the importance of a people's cultural
and social milieu. They are proud of the fact that they are not culture bound, at
least no more than some people and certainly far less than most people, and that
they have the techniques and empathy and a remarkable adaptability which helps
them to blend fairly easily into almost any cultural landscape. In short they believe that they can combine the methodology of science, the introspection of the
artist, and the concerns of the humanist. They also believe that their respect for
the people among whom they live and work gives them a unique insight into
cultures very different from their own (Lévi-Strauss 1966). If they show respect,
and elect to participate as far as possible in local affairs, they can shed the stigma

and suspicions attached to an intruding stranger which can so badly mar the relations between a guest and his hosts. Of course, anthropologists accept the fact that they are not free from subtle prejudices, stereotypical attitudes, narrowly circumscribed social customs, an ethnocentric view of the "good life," or inflexible political opinions, and that idiosyncratic features of their personalities sometimes get in the way of relations with their equally varied informants. A number of anthropologists (Gutkind, Jongmans, Jonker and Serpenti, 1967), but far too few, have candidly discussed the implications of these more negative features but have stressed the efforts they have made to overcome them (Bowen 1954; Malinowski 1967; Powdermaker 1966).

We also know that anthropologists, particularly those who have worked in Africa, have generally worked in a colonial milieu (Colson 1967; Gough 1968). Indeed, most of us who worked in Africa in the years before independence realized that our research was carried out under the protective umbrella of colonial administrations and their officers (Maquet 1964); anthropologists were, Maquet writes, "not assimilated into the African layer of the [colonial] society. They were members of the white minority" (p. 48). Upon arrival in an African country, the anthropologist was well advised to clear his credentials and objectives first with the local European administrative officer, who then introduced him to the local chief, elders, council members, or other community leaders. While few anthropologists considered this an ideal introduction to a community about which they knew little as yet, they had little choice but to accept the authority of the colonial administration. It was this authority which, initially at least, structured the relationship between the anthropologist and his informants and created the social distance between the "white" anthropologist and his "African" informants—particularly if the latter had been drawn into the preindependence anticolonial political struggle. Race, in many African countries, became the sole determinant of relationship between black and white. Diamond (1964:143), reflecting on exactly such a situation, writes:

> Still I shuddered at being stereotyped and forced to share a guilt that I felt had been personally expunged by training, insight, and sympathy. My mode of life, my opportunities, the very clothes I wore were an insult to these disinherited. From a social distance, anthropologist, colonial administrator, business man seemed alike. From a greater distance, only the color of the skin was visible, and beyond that any man on the social horizon might be an enemy.
>
> Colonizing civilization had created these distances; good intentions were merely precious and sentiments cheap. The Africans who called out to me in town were no better than I. But once human hatred finds an affective occasion and a plausible excuse in the repression and inequities of civilization, it is implacable.

Diamond (1964:144-145) goes on to point out how race, conquest, and trade are intimately interwoven:

> Cultures have been ruined for the sake of modern mercantilism, and societies conquer so as to secure unimpeded trade. Millions of people, stimulated to produce for the Europeans in little lots that converged to enormous shipments, bought back, in towns like Jos, some small expensive thing that seemed cheap because of

its size or inferior quality. Tiny individual measures of production and consumption, but they commanded all the surplus sinew and strength of British West Africa. No wonder Europeans were uneasy around Jos. The "white man bastard" was the unseen presence, the invisible master. He rarely materialized; his goods stood up for him. Conquest by trade was indirect conquest; indirect conquest was best served by indirect rule.

Lévi-Strauss (1966:126) too puts the matter unequivocally:

Anthropology is not a dispassionate science like astronomy, which springs from the contemplation of things at a distance. It is the outcome of a historical process which has made the larger part of mankind subservient to the other, and during which millions of human beings have had their resources plundered and their institutions and beliefs destroyed, whilst they themselves were ruthlessly killed, thrown into bondage, and contaminated by diseases they were unable to resist. Anthropology is daughter to this era of violence: its capacity to assess more objectively the facts pertaining to the human condition reflects, on the epistomological level, a state of affairs in which one part of mankind treated the other as an object.

This context then, as to a large extent now, strongly influenced the attitudes of both African informants, colonial administrators, and nowadays, African governments toward the anthropologist and his professional activities. Diamond (1964:153) summarizes the anthropologist's dilemma:

Logically enough, anthropologists are frequently taken as spies because of the inquisitive nature of their work, their concern with local affairs in remote places to which they go, their tendency to fade into the background of local custom in living up to the canons of participant observation. They have, also, a certain limited academic immunity; they travel freely, and what better cover could a secret agent desire. A logical case can be constructed, and often has been, against any anthropologist in the field almost anywhere in this era of active and reactive crises that echo to the uttermost ends of the earth. Of course, in the spiritual sense anthropologists are Kierkegaardian double agents. That is, engaged in a search for the varieties of human experience, they are marginal to the commercial-industrial society that created them; and they are transient, if eager, participants elsewhere. Anthropology is a scholarly discipline, but it is also a kind of secretly structured revolt, a search for human possibilities. Police agents, who are known for their theological sensitivity, instinctually suspect that sort of thing.

Then, as now, anthropologists were torn by many conflicts, both personal and professional (Gough 1968). They have, however, always felt a strong sense of loyalty to the people and their institutions to which they attached themselves in the course of their fieldwork. While few contemporary anthropologists will expose in their writing a sense of paternalism or possessiveness, or a romantic idealization of the "primitive," in the course of conversation it is not unusual to hear references to "my people," "my tribe," or "the people in my village." To most anthropologists such expressions are devoid of the negative connotations which many African leaders and intellectuals attribute to them (Gutkind 1967). Rather they see these sentiments as evidence of their personal loyalties to their informants and also, as

Diamond pointed out, "a search for human possibilities." These sentiments and attitudes not infrequently produce conflicts in the professional realm, such as those concerning the contents, the scope, orientation, purpose, and function of anthropology and its subdisciplines.

Clearly, today, anthropology is in the eye of a major storm which rotates around both the theoretical and practical contribution which it can make to a broadly based social science. Furthermore, the subject matter of anthropology, reasonably small-scale and relatively homogeneous preliterate and non-Western societies, is rapidly being transformed into modern nation states of their components. To some observers, anthropology must either radically transform itself or be satisfied with being no more than a salvage operation to retrieve as much of the "exotic" as can still be obtained. In view of the past concerns of anthropologists, "it is not surprising," Audrey Richards (1961:4) writes, "that anthropology should now appear to many people to be a kind of anachronism, hopelessly inadequate as a type of research and likely to be blown off the field, like so much else, by the famous winds of change." The anthropologist finds it ever more difficult to seek out a "tribe" which has not been "studied" by anyone, or about which we still know very little because the only information we have about it is what an administrator or missionary wrote some fifty years before.

> If tribal cultural differences are to be regretted, discouraged and even denied it is not unnatural that African governments, old and new, view the financing of a series of tribal studies without much enthusiasm, even in cases where no previous account of one of the major cultural groups in a territory exists. World financiers are unlikely to wait for three year studies of even important tribes before plunging into widespread schemes for the development of old or newly independent territories.... The Governments of East Africa tended to ask for research on problems rather than peoples. (Richards 1961:5)

However, the relevant issue is not really whether or not anthropologists and anthropology will shift from a narrow interest in tribal studies to a major concern with comparative social change and modernization, from anthropology to comparative sociology, as Radcliffe-Brown might have suggested—rather, it is that anthropologists must recognize that whatever the tasks they now tackle, whatever the group of people and institutions they have selected for concentrated study, their work demands from them an understanding that Africans, and other peoples in the low-income world, are now part of a complex political, economic, and social network which reaches not only deeply beyond tribal boundaries but also into world society at large. What we witness today is the eclipse of tribal societies, in traditionalist terms, and the rise of societies based on district, regional, and national foundations. Abstractly conceived, this might be denied by those who, in the words of Gluckman, have been "reared on the rural tradition of the tribe," but on closer inspection few Africans are outside the growing influence of new political structures; many are part of new associations such as trade unions or producer or marketing cooperatives; many Africans are now linked so intimately with rapidly increasing urban areas; and above all few Africans can escape the pervading influence of education, a proliferation of new choices and styles of life, or the penetration of Western influences, be they economic or ideational. In this sense, the anthropologist as fieldworker is faced with increasingly complicated decisions in defining exactly the unit of his observations. Of course, such a formulation does not exclude the possibility, or even the desirability, of carrying out traditionalist tribal studies, for after all, as Richards has put it, African cultures are as worthy of study "as others in our universe" (1961:7). Dr. Richards has made a strong plea for "a continuous series of tribal studies . . . focused on important political or economic problems" and presented in a comparative frame of reference (Richards 1961:10). However, we must remember that societies have changed far more rapidly than anthropologists have (Lévi-Strauss 1966). It is the people of Africa, Asia, and Latin America who are setting the pace. The question is, can we keep up with them?

A start has been made. After all it has been the anthropologist who has pioneered urban research, studies of local government, labor problems, land tenure, myriad problems in family life, the shift from subsistence to cash cropping, the rise of new forms of executive authority, and the implications of unemployment. However, anthropologists have not always felt at ease in the macrosetting of major institutional transformation because they have been burdened with assumptions about the organization and operation of traditional social systems. These assumptions have reflected some rather subtle stereotyped impressions some of us have held, that small-scale and preliterate societies are "simple" or "backward," or that the natural habitat for Africans is rurality. Hence, rapid change is disruptive. Thus, in the rural context we have been able to show that "membership of a tribe involves participation in a working political system, and sharing of domestic life with kinsfolk" (Gluckman 1961:67); and that the operation of social organization is based on a structure of interlocking corporateness which exhibits repetitive and, hence, predictive patterns. While we have not always committed ourselves on paper, we have assumed that the urban situation was radically different, that is, that social organization had an amorphous quality and that social disorganization and anomie impeded integration. Some observers took this view simply because the African urban population was a complex composite of varied tribal groups— a group of people not bound by a common tradition, language, habits, and ideas. Studies of urban Africa over the last fifteen years have indicated beyond doubt, however, that "urban life exhibits sufficient regularities for us to extract systematic inter-connections which we can arrange to exhibit a structure, and we can show how this structure changes" (Gluckman 1961:68). What is required as a "starting point for analysis of urbanization must be an urban system of relations, in which the tribal origins of the population may even be regarded as of secondary interest. . . . We have to start with a theory about urban systems" (Gluckman 1961: 80).

What I am trying to indicate here is that while societies have changed, particularly African societies, neither anthropologists nor their methodologies have changed as rapidly. Thus, when an anthropologist decides to work in one of Africa's urban areas, he is faced with a fieldwork situation totally different from past field experiences in a rural area or, should this be his first fieldwork, he finds that the literature on anthropological fieldwork method appears to have little relevance in an urban context (Gutkind 1967). Not only do urban areas differ significantly in composition, size and institutional structure from rural social systems, but the relationships between fieldworkers and informants differ. It is this which I wish to discuss now in some detail.

I indicated earlier that in the last few years Africans have progressively found themselves enmeshed in political and economic networks whose purposes and operations are largely determined by structures larger and more complex than the conditions which determine rural-based tribal life. African urbanites in particular live in societies which mirror these developments. In urban areas, and in the population as a whole, are to be found virtually all the manifestations of transformation and modernization, defining the former as a continuous dynamic process whereby a total social and cultural configuration is gradually rearranged, and modernization as "the will to be modern," to deliberately and actively plan change, to be scientific and to apply rationality to a planning process. Even more so, the urban areas give us a very clear indication of how individual and group relations are being restructured; how new associations come into being; how new political and economic alliances are being made; how conflicts arise and are being mediated; how integration takes place around variables which in the past we have not associated with this potential; and how African society has become, and continues to be, internally differentiated as a result of education, ideational, and technological change resulting in differential access to political and economic power. The urban areas in Africa are the pace setters of change (Gutkind 1962), and their residents are like a barometer sensitively reflecting almost all aspects of the micro- and macrotransformation taking place. As economic and social distance widens between the elite (here broadly defined as the self-employed, the wage earners, and the salaried) and the poor, a conflict of interest is generated, which is perhaps inherent in modernization and national development, affecting all sections of the new African nations—but it is in the urban areas that we see this conflict most clearly. It is conventional to analyze this class of conflicting interests, and the struggle by individuals and groups to find a niche in a new political, economic, and social order, in the context of the "tensions" of development. The poor in urban Africa reflect the problems and tensions of this development, and also the response and adaptation to change and modernization.

II

While very few urban anthropologists have told us of the problems they encountered during their fieldwork, or how they overcame them, there is little doubt that the anthropologist's initial contact with his urban informants is often rather unsettling. Thus, when I arrived in Lagos and had cleared my credentials with the Ministry of Labour of the (then) Military Government (June–July 1966), I was introduced to the supervisors of the Ikoyi Employment Exchange. On my arrival I was immediately surrounded by a large number of men, at least fifty, who had lined up outside the Exchange. In rapid fire succession, several men asked me whether I had come to hire them. As rapidly, testimonials and certificates were pressed into my hands while the torrent of comments and questions continued, and at the same time the numbers surrounding me grew. It took some time for me to quiet them so I could listen to one speaker at a time, while those men whose papers I had in my hand assumed that I had immediately shown a special interest in them.[1] One of them grabbed my arm and suggested that I go elsewhere to talk with him. Not only was it virtually impossible for me to break through the tight circle around me but I had to explain to this eager man that I must first listen to what others had to say. This discouraged him and he left the group grumbling and complaining that he had lost his place in the line outside the office and that his name might have been called to present his labor card. Others also left to regain their places, leaving only about thirty men.

I suggested to this group that we should move away so as not to interfere with the operation of the Exchange. We moved to a large tree nearby and were joined by a local policeman who had crossed the street to find out about the agitation and the shouting. No sooner had we gathered near the tree than a group of younger, better-dressed men, who had been waiting some distance from the main office, joined us. I learned later that they were junior secondary school leavers who rarely mixed with the unskilled and unschooled who comprised the bulk of the applicants. These younger men stood aside but close enough to hear what was being said. For the time being they took no part in the conversation, but I was once again surrounded by at least fifty men. As I looked around I could tell that many hundreds of men, and a few young girls, were casting eyes in my direction, while many of those who obviously gathered each morning at a windowless barnlike structure behind the Exchange had come forward. Some of the labor officers were looking out of their offices, wondering what was taking place.

I sat down on a low concrete wall close to the tree and asked those nearest me to do likewise and those in front of me to sit on the grass. Some did but others persisted in standing and looked suspiciously and a little menacingly at me. After a few moments, during which the policeman moved up to the front, an older man asked me what I had come to do. I carefully explained to him, while also addressing others near me, that I had come to learn as much as I could about the life and problems of the unemployed. I told them that I had worked for some years in African towns and that this was my second visit to Nigeria. In the summer of 1964 I had traveled extensively in West and East Africa to learn from government officials and those working in universities why many men were unable to find work. At that moment I was interrupted by a very tall young man who had stood apart a little all along and who asked whether I had come to give him work. A man closer by took up the question and repeated it several times while others began to talk with each other. The policeman raised his hands a little and asked everyone

---

[1] Most of the primary, and certainly all the secondary, school leavers had a good working command of English. It was surprising what a large number of even the unschooled had picked up enough Engish to allow me to interview them—I had no knowledge of any of the Nigerian languages. While my three research assistants (two Ibos, one Yoruba), all college graduates, carried out interviews in the vernacular (that is, in Ibo, Yoruba, or Hausa) when called upon to do so, I experienced very few difficulties in my own interviewing. The questionnaires which I eventually used were, however, in English, Yoruba, Ibo, or Hausa.

to be silent. He also stepped back a little to speak to one man who was trying to push his way to the front.

Rather than turn to the person who had asked me the question, I turned to the group as a whole, explaining again that I had come from a university in Canada to learn as much as I could from the unemployed about how they managed their affairs. I was not, I explained carefully, able to give them work, although if I did hear about any opportunities I would notify the supervisor of the Labour Exchange. This last comment stimulated several men to shout a hearty "No!" I asked why and was told by a person sitting next to me that if I heard about any job opportunities I should tell the men about it first. But why, I asked, was it not fairer to all that those who had waited for work longest should get the first chance? Several men wanted to speak all at once so that again it was impossible to make out what was being said. The policeman, edging his way closer to me and now facing the crowd, called for order. He had come, he explained, to help me (because, as I learned later, his brother, a trade union organizer, had once visited Canada in a training program).

A man in his late twenties, who had acted in a rather aggressive and agitated way, moved forward to speak. He said that he had worked as a timekeeper for a construction company, but when the work was finished he had lost his job. He pointed to his clothes and to those of others, which were rather ragged, and said that he had been without work for over two years. He had come every day to the Exchange (at that moment he showed me his labor registration card, while others were also pulling theirs from their pockets) and waited "with all my many friends" to be called; but he was never called, and he was tired of waiting. If I knew of any job, I should go to him and his friends "because I can organize my friends," and tell them about it. It was wrong for me, he went on, to give such information to the labor officers because they would merely use this to their own advantage.

This last reference was clearly a signal because many men nodded their agreement, while others shouted their support. The theme was taken up by a man who had meandered over to the group. He was pushing a cycle, was fairly well-dressed, and identified himself as a driver. He said that I clearly did not understand anything about "our misery" because I would have known that the only way to get work was to pay some money to the labor officers or the politicians. As the group nodded their approval, he went on to tell me that only those Europeans who had jobs to offer were welcome at the Exchange. A lot of people at the back of the Exchange, he explained, had just been told that a European had come to hire workers; he now realized that this was not so, that I had merely come to talk with them and to ask them questions, but their problems were not my business. Was I working for the government or the police, he asked? Another man in the crowd suggested that they were all wasting their time. And why was the policeman there, he asked? Still another man said that if I could not find work for them, I had better go away to the "Bristol Hotel" where most rich visitors stayed.

The policeman had clearly tired of the conversation; he pushed his way through the crowd and left. Others, too, left, and those who stayed behind showed little further interest in my presence. They began to smoke and engage in conversation among themselves, while some walked over to a women selling bread rolls.

As the men drifted away, three young men came over to me. They were part of a group of over twenty junior secondary school leavers. They had watched me closely but had not taken part in the conversation. The person who started off the conversation was immaculately dressed, wearing a tie and well-pressed trousers. He asked me what I was doing and whether he could help me. I repeated my explanation and said that indeed I would enjoy talking with him and his friends. At this he motioned to the others, who drifted over to us; those who had been with me earlier all walked off laughing and frequently looking behind to see what I was doing.

The conversation began with Utuk, a nineteen-year-old Ibo from a village in the (then) eastern region of Nigeria. He claimed that he had to give up his schooling in Onitsha because he had five younger brothers and sisters and they, too, needed school fees. His father, a farmer, could not support them all and his other relatives who had helped him and others in the past could assist no longer. He had come to Lagos seven months before to live with his mother's brother who owned a small printing business in Lagos. His uncle had offered him an apprenticeship in his business, but Utuk had turned this down, hoping he could get office work. In the first two months of his stay in Lagos, he wrote many letters to government departments, commercial houses, and industries. He claimed to have written some sixty-eight applications in over five months, but had not been called for an interview. In the third month he registered at the Employment Exchange and appeared there three times a week. On the other days he either stayed at home, visited his friends, or wrote more applications. Sometimes he went to the movies, watched horseracing, or walked about the streets looking at shops, but, he explained, most of the time "I must help my uncle and his wife in their house." He said that he felt rather discouraged because a week ago he had had a quarrel with his uncle, who had warned him that unless he found a job soon he would have to return to his village or move on to another relative. Utuk said that he objected to being turned into a servant with his education!

Others near us took up this theme at some length. A number of them related their experiences during long periods of unemployment ranging from seven months to three years. Some had casual jobs, which they mostly disliked, but others had lived without independent means in the homes of relatives and friends. Some had shown greater initiative in obtaining employment than others, such as coming to the Exchange every day or tramping the streets from one office to the next, but all of them lived in the hope of getting a lucky break. One young man explained that it was impossible for them to return to their homes because they did not want to dig the land, and in any case their relatives expected them to earn some money so they could make their own contribution to the family effort. Another chipped in to say, after looking around the group first, that it was "bad" for Ibos not to be able to look after themselves; Ibos worked harder "than other people," but they also "know how to look after each other."

I asked them why they thought they were unemployed and why there was a shortage of jobs. After some discussion they agreed on three reasons. First, you had to know a person of high political and economic office to help you secure work. Second, there were not enough businesses and factories in Lagos and the other large towns in Nigeria. Third, only a small group of people had benefited from independence and most political leaders and other important men considered those beneath them with contempt: "They only cared for themselves and the money they could make," added one young chap, while others mentioned several federal and regional government ministers killed in the coup of January 1966 or dismissed from office since.

After some more discussion on these subjects, several of these young men turned to me wanting to know more about me, my work, and "what I could do" for them. Once again I explained to the best of my ability what I was doing in Lagos (and that I would repeat this in Nairobi later), and that I had neither knowledge about the job market nor any contacts or authority to help them obtain employment. I was, I explained, a research worker and that the prerequisite for action, that is how more jobs are to be found for people, was to have as much information as possible about the problems of unemployment and the unemployed.

Initially, this simple explanation seemed to satisfy them. However, after a little more casual and jovial conversation, one young man suggested that "there is a lot wrong with this country" and that if I ever wanted to understand what was wrong I had better listen to *them* rather than to government officials and the politicians. Indeed, this is what I had been told a little earlier. The same person suggested that the "most important contribution" I could make to the solution of their problem was to expose all the bribery and corruption that went on. I told him that when I came across evidence which was unquestionably proven, I would include this information in the writing up of my work. Another person asked how much travel I had done in Nigeria and whether I would only speak to the uneducated. He asked me to tell them what I had been told by the many men who had "captured" me when I first arrived at the Exchange, saying that I had better be careful before I believed all that I was told by these men. Most of them, he added, were lazy, had no skills, and would do anything just for a shilling. Also, they were always fighting with each other and some consulted witch doctors, believing this was the surest way to get work. Another person, who had thus far taken no part in the conversation, asked me how I could convince them that I was trustworthy. I had, after all, asked them to help me in my work. I found this difficult to answer and merely indicated that gradually they would get to know me. This same person said that he had asked me this because he had known other Europeans who had not really liked Africans. Some of them treated Africans like children, but when they needed information they did not reveal their "private" thoughts. He thought that Nigeria might be better off without the Europeans. He had seen many of them drive big cars and live in big houses. He had never seen a European without work; if there were any, they would surely come to the Employment Exchange. Some of his teachers had told him that the European way of life was best and that the sooner they learned this way of life the better off they would be. At that moment a young chap protested with some anger that they had "learned the European way of life," but that they were no better off.

Utuk, with whom my conversation with these school leavers had begun, had kept silent for quite some time. He now became quite agitated and asked me what I thought was a better life: to live in the village or the city. I replied that it depended on the choice that a person made and that some people liked to live on the land and others preferred the town. Some asked me whether I lived in a village and did I like it, or did I live in a city "and could do what [I] liked?" I told them that I lived in a big city—the city of Montreal—but that I had also lived in African villages. To this Utuk replied: "Then you must know that the villages are dead. All of us," he went on, "prefer to live in Lagos because there is no work in the villages." Others were more specific and told me that their education entitled them to live in the city. But, I asked them, what if they would not find work in Lagos —would they eventually return to the village? Without looking around at each other, they replied with a firm "no." Utuk took up the conversation again, saying that "to go back to the village is to suffer and perhaps to perish."

At that moment a labor officer came over to us and called out a name of a young man who had said nothing throughout our conversation. He followed him to the office. The others looked with interest over to the Exchange and some walked over casually to find out why their friend had been called. This was indeed the end of our conversation, as most of the young men left. I decided to go home.

III

That night I reflected on what I had experienced. My initial "encounter," I thought, had been rather stormy. There were many strands of thought which whizzed through my mind. However, my interests and concerns were more with what was revealed in this encounter *in terms of my future field relations* with the unemployed than, at that moment, with the vast range of superficial information which I had obtained in just under three hours. While much of what I had heard gave me pointers for future exploration, I had no way of knowing how representative were the views thrown at me. It seemed to me, at the time, that I had elected to work in a very explosive political and personal situation and I wondered, quite seriously, whether I could face up to the pressures which seemed to lie ahead. For a moment a vivid picture came to my mind of the men who had pressed references and testimonials into my hands, who had begged me for work, whom I had seen sitting dejectedly on the grass and of those who had aggressively demanded that I provide them with work. I felt a momentary wave of fear and helplessness. For the next few weeks I was to work among men who would put me under intense pressure to "do something for them," but this I was unable to do. This pressure was not, of course, totally new to me. All anthropologists experience this in some measure (Williams 1967), and it invariably raises a conflict between professional demands and personal inclinations. Nor was it strange that on arrival I was surrounded by a group of people who questioned me about my purpose and attitudes. Yet the intensity of this encounter was new. Here, I was to work among a group of men whose political sentiments and economic and social position made them highly sensitive, angry, cynical, and suspicious. All strangers find themselves in this position, but, it appeared to me, few anthropologists become, within minutes of arrival in the field, the targets for a release of tension and an outpouring of opinions and attitudes; had I become the kicking post whereby my informants would blame me for all that struck them as wrong in Nigeria?

At the time it seemed to me that I faced two new situations. First, I reflected on the change in the context for the social researcher. In the colonial context, the relationship between the social researcher and the informants had been something of a patron-client relationship (Colson 1967) of submission, subservience, and ingratiation, all of which reflected the variables of political domination, race, and social distance. Since independence, although this is perhaps too sharp a distinction, the social researcher is faced with an aggressive assertion of rights and privileges, and an exposé of aspirations and hope, not all realized with political independence. The anthropologist now stands alone; gone are the days when behind him stood the force of the Provincial Commissioner and his administrative officers. Of course, I am not suggesting that the anthropologist was a colonialist in mind and action (although, no doubt, some enjoyed the colonial atmosphere), but rather that he was part of a total system of political and social relations which carried with it high status—however unjustified this might have been. The situation has changed. The colonial administrators have yielded to a politically and socially sensitive African civil service, suspicious of foreign scholars; and the villagers have moved into an urban community being rapidly proletarianized. Reasonable homogeneity of the village has been replaced by the extreme heterogeneity of the cities and towns; and above all, African society now shows all the features, both structural and ideational, of a class system—however incipient at present.

Second, my brief encounter had taught me a lesson which I could not forget, that my research topic could not be defined in narrow terms. The reason was simple: The unemployed would not let me. I came into the field with an interest in the social organization among the unemployed living in Lagos. How did they look after themselves, or who looked after them? How did they set about finding employment? How did various ethnic groups use the rules of traditional reciprocity? I realized, however, that these questions, and many others, were rooted in far more complex matters of macroeconomic and political change, and that many aspects of modernization and national development would have to be considered. I was glad that I had set out to do no more than a "pilot" study! I also began to ask myself, in panic rather than with deliberate reason, whether I should quickly read some of the major texts on theories of economic development and political transformation. However, having recently read Gluckman's *Closed Systems and Open Minds: The Limits of Naivety in Social Anthropology* (1964), I was filled with all the fears that I would have to "trespass," "circumscribe," and "abridge" a vast amount of data over which I had little command and whose relevance I might never clearly see. I wondered, however, with a sense of the pioneer, could I blaze the trail of a new social anthropology with a broader outlook, purpose, and sense of problems?

Also, at the time, I was quite uncertain what methodological techniques I could use. Would my African informants answer my questions despite initial hostility? All anthropologists, however, ask themselves the same question, yet eventually they find at least a few informants willing to involve themselves. Yet the villager, I falsely argued, was surely a captive informant whose actions one could observe even if no face-to-face communication was possible. Would the unemployed just turn away from me into the urban mass, never to be found again? While I wanted to talk to them, they wanted work. Would I be able to keep a balanced intellectual and emotional attitude when being pressed by hundreds of men pleading real (but at times also fictitious) need? How would I respond to a situation in which my work would be constantly interrupted by demands for favors? Here again I realized that sociologists working in slum areas must have had similar problems and found ways to adjust to such circumstances.

How would I select a sample from the unemployed which would in the least be representative of a very diverse group? Should I work intensively with few or extensively with many? While it is clearly false to assume that having studied one village of a tribe it is possible to generalize about other villages, I was very conscious of the difficulties in presenting a reasonably representative picture of the unemployed.[2] I was also greatly concerned about my ability to cross the enormous economic barrier which separated me from my informants. The unemployed had expressed to me strong views of what they thought of those who "ride in big cars," live in "big houses," and look down on them. To escape this sentiment, should I walk or ride a bicycle? Yet I drove a car, and whenever I arrived at the Labour Exchange I was besieged by an army of young men willing to wash it!

Not least of my worries that night were questions about the political sensitivity of the government, which had earlier expressed concern to me about the possible consequences of research among the unemployed. Senior officers in the Ministry of Labour, Lagos, had questioned me very closely about the objectives of my research. Each one of them had given me to understand that while unemployment existed, serious attention was being given to possible solutions. It was also impressed upon me that the consequences of unemployment were not as serious for an African as they had been for a European before unemployment compensation schemes were initiated. In addition, I was cautioned on several occasions not to believe the complaints I would hear about nepotism, tribalistic sentiments, corrupt practices, elitism, favoritism, and other charges designed to discredit the civil service, that is, specifically the labor officers. Strong steps would be taken, I was informed, should the Minister of Labour ever find that such charges were proven. Complaints and disturbances, I was told, came from a very small minority

---

[2] In this essay I have paid no attention to problems of methodology because I want to concentrate on the theme of this publication: stress and response in fieldwork. However, a brief note on field procedures is appropriate.

My interest was in the social life of the unemployed, not in the etiology or extent of unemployment. Thus, my first efforts were designed to get some idea of who the unemployed were, that is, to establish ten major categories using the dimensions of age, education, and skills. My next step was to collect one-hundred life histories, ten from each of these categories. I worked on these life histories for four weeks; then I began to design a pilot questionnaire, which I pretested five times, each time rephrasing questions and format. The questionnaires were uncoded because only one-hundred men were involved (and another one-hundred in Nairobi) and also because I found it difficult to specify response categories which would accommodate all the subtleties in the replies. I viewed the questionnaire technique as no more than a supplement to intensive interviewing, observation, and participation. I made no rigorous attempt at sampling, a problem still to be tackled.

of people, mostly those who were lazy, who were unemployable, who refused to accept jobs commensurate with their education, had personal grudges against anyone and everyone, and were "professional agitators." The police knew about the latter, and the government was getting tired of those who steadily interfered with the efforts being made to assist those who "genuinely" needed work.

With such information I felt a little uneasy, wondering why a policeman might have watched the day's proceedings with such interest. As my work unfolded during the next two months, I considered it of prime importance to answer every question from officials about my work with complete honesty, an approach which I believe was not only professionally and morally correct but also rewarding in the information I obtained and the access to documentation permitted me. Yet I fully protected the anonymity of my informants and at no stage was I asked to act otherwise. I had no reason to believe that over time any of my informants ever seriously doubted that my objective was to carry out objective research and that this required that I maintain cordial and cooperative relations with many individuals. For the unemployed this implied their recognition that I felt sympathetic to their problems, and that if I could have helped them I would have done so, and to the administrator it was clear that I was not committed to work against their interests and plans.

In retrospect, I realized how my initial encounter had not only thrown up a great deal of information but also sensitized me to many real (and, no doubt, also some imaginary) problems associated with a tense situation. I looked forward with considerable anticipation to my work the next day. While I recognized the problems ahead, I was also a little recklessly determined to overcome these because my time in Lagos was limited to two months. Thus, at times I thought I was pressing informants too hard as I saw many of them day after day. Sometimes I had to pull myself up very sharply to restrict probing tangential, though important, areas. I talked with economists and political scientists, manpower research experts, and social service administrators, politicians, and labor leaders. I felt that each one of them had a particular insight and analyzed the social and economic situation of the unemployed with different perspectives. Many a time I was admonished that my perspectives would completely distort "the facts." More frequently than anything else, I was asked, "What kind of anthropologist are you?" Because few of my questioners allowed me time to explain my ideas and approaches, they generally assumed that I was really seeking information about the "primitive" African under the disguise of an interest in the unemployed. On at least five occasions Nigerian academics questioned me about the sources of my financial support, and more frequently yet some of my Nigerian colleagues jokingly asked me whether I was working for the Royal Canadian Mounted Police. All these were responses new to me, and the very nature of their ambiguity was always a little unsettling. However, the very intense pressure of work pushed many of these thoughts into the background. Once involved in fieldwork, particularly in a politically tense situation, it gathers momentum and proceeds without a sagging intertia.

To conclude: As yet, I have no major generalizations to suggest which might have wider applicability. Nor do I wish to put forward hypotheses which might be useful for testing elsewhere. The reason for this reluctance is that I have restricted myself to a description of a single and momentary situation, all of whose implications I was unable to follow through in any great depth. Nor was I certain that I had drawn the correct conclusions from initial observations and experiences. However, that night I looked back to some of the highlights of my fieldwork experiences dating back to 1953, when I arrived in Kampala, Uganda. I was to work in a periurban area, a heterogeneous and fairly congested area (Southall and Gutkind 1957) to which Africans had drifted in large numbers after the war in response to the new labor demands generated by a new tempo in economic development. I also recalled that I was eased into the situation very gradually. Then one of my first interests was to try to understand a "colonial" situation, both historically and in its contemporary dimensions, and how this situation had imposed itself on Uganda as a whole. I was also concerned with how I might fit into a colonial dominated society and how I would respond to working among the economically complex and politically and socially sophisticated Ganda (the dominant ethnic group in and around Kampala) whose style of life had often generated rather ambivalent attitudes toward them among fieldworkers.

However, the lesson I learned in Lagos, which prepared me more effectively for my work two months later in Nairobi, was simple: In a contemporary fieldwork situation in Africa the social researcher, particularly one concerned with questions of change and modernization, is almost immediately exposed to a wide range of complex data which reflect the multiplex problems of national development. Furthermore, the fieldworker now working in independent African countries is exposed to, and becomes involved in, the tensions which reflect the social, economic, and political transformation. In a sense the use by the social researcher of the participant observation technique shades delicately into the social researcher as participant. If these observations are correct, then the implications both in terms of "Problemstellung" and methodology are clearly far-reaching.

3

Stress and Strategy
in Three Field Situations

FRANCES HENRY

THE NATURE OF A research problem and the context in which the research is undertaken affect the general strategy of fieldwork and the methods of data collection employed by the researcher. My aim in this chapter is to describe the various methodological procedures which I used in carrying out three separate research studies and to examine some of the factors which influenced the kinds of data collected, the conditions under which it was collected, and the various and differing roles asumed in order to contact and to establish rapport with informants. I will also discuss briefly the kinds of problems encountered during the course of these studies and my attempts at solving them.

I

I first came to Trinidad, West Indies, in 1956 with the intention of doing a study of an Afro-American religious cult, the members of which call themselves "Shango" or "Orisha" people. An earlier study of a Negro Pentescostal Church undertaken for an M.A. thesis led to an interest in New World Negro religious movements. In reading the literature, I discovered that such groups were found in many areas of the Caribbean and particularly in Haiti, where a well-developed African-based religious system—Vodun—is practiced by the majority of the population. In view of my very limited familiarity with Creole, the Haitian language, I decided instead to investigate the Shango cult in Trinidad, then a British Crown Colony and therefore English speaking. I intended to describe the belief system of the cult; the nature and extent of its religious activities; its social organization, recruitment, and leadership patterns, and one of its most important means of religious expression, spirit possession.

I had no particular research design in mind before my arrival in Trinidad and assumed that I would be using the traditional techniques of anthropology—

35

participant observation and both structured and unstructured interviews. The cult had not been studied systematically and therefore little ethnographic information was available to me. Upon arrival in Trinidad, my first job was to find the center or centers of cult activities and some people who belonged to it. This proved more difficult than anticipated. Casual questioning of taxi drivers and the like in Port of Spain, the capital city, brought no results. Some people knew vaguely about the cult, but could not tell me where in the city or in the island it was located. I soon realized by gradually meeting members of the Trinidadian middle class that, although they knew little about cult activities, they were nevertheless quick to condemn such religious practices as being "African" and therefore barbaric.[1] I was often told that very few people actually belonged to the cult, and that Trinidadians were, by and large, a Christian people. One or two French Creoles (locally born whites of French descent) suggested that I study a Christian community or any other problem which did not involve their negatively evaluated "black" African heritage. Despite such attempts to dissuade me from my purpose, I continued the search for the Shango followers.

On the hunch that cult members were also involved in physical and psychological healing practices, I consulted with the director of the mental hospital, who encouraged the study but could offer little help in finding cult members. A number of government officials were cooperative and very useful in supplying me with information on the history of the legislation which, until 1947, prohibited cult activity. One government official arranged an introduction to a local "folklorist" who thought a cult center was located "somewhere" in the hills surrounding Port of Spain. He accompanied me on several trips into that area and we were finally told by a shopkeeper that a center was located on a particular road. As this happened late in the afternoon, we arranged to go there on the following day, but an urgent matter detained my friend and I decided to try to find the center on my own. I went by taxi to the road and walked up and down, making inquiries at several houses until I found the home and ceremonial compound of a cult leader. By this time, I was eager to begin research since I had been in the country for three weeks. In retrospect, this is a relatively short time to establish contact with the research group and many fieldworkers spend considerably more time in getting located, but to me, at the time, it seemed an eternity. In my eagerness and inexperience, I perhaps violated one of the cardinal rules of fieldwork procedure in that I walked into the leader's compound entirely alone and without an official introduction from a local "contact" person. Although at that time the Shango group was unused to visitors, I was welcomed warmly by "Tanti," the cult leader. I explained that I was a student from North America particularly interested in religion, that I had heard about Shango, but that no one seemed to know much about it, and that I wanted to observe their religious activities and talk to some of the members. In a country where the lower-class population is renowned for its re-

---

[1] Trinidad was, and to some extent still is, a highly class-color stratified society; the elites are either foreign or locally born "whites," the middle class mainly brown skinned and recently mobile, and the predominant group in the population are lower-class blacks. Slightly more than a third of the population derives from India, and these people are mainly Hindu, Moslem, and Christian. Indians rarely participate in African-based religions.

ligious fervor, her attention was immediately drawn to my interest in religious behavior. Almost immediately after presenting myself, she told me at great length about how people were "backsliding," "sinning," and immoral. I returned the following day and was introduced to some of her followers. She invited me to her "feast" which, fortunately, was due in a week's time. I attended this feast and met there a number of other prominent cult leaders.

Under the continued patronage of Tanti, I gradually made myself and my presence known to other leaders, drummers, and members involved in cult activities. It soon became apparent that there were cult centers, each under the direction of a leader, in many areas of the island and that a major feast (which lasts for four days and nights) was held by each leader in turn—most taking place during my summer field period. This particular Shango group (and there were others, as I later discovered) was integrated into a formal network of about ten to twelve leaders and their immediate followers, all of whom were trained by the head or "king" of the Shango worshippers. As each leader held a feast, the members would travel to his compound, settle in, and live there for the duration of the feast. At a particular feast many spectators and occasional participants were drawn from the immediate area in which the cult leader lived and attended usually only the local feast in that area, but the hard core of leaders and active participants traveled from one to another in a fairly continuous round of feast activity. During this active feast period, I traveled along and saw at least twenty feasts. I was able to record notes on behavioral observation during both possessed and nonpossessed states. Most of my interviewing was done informally during the days when the women were mainly engaged in cooking. During the actual ceremony, particularly during quiet periods, I was easily able to engage onlookers in conversations, and there were always small groups of people in various parts of the compound who were willing to talk to me. Between feast periods, I would travel to the various compounds of other leaders in order to interview them and their immediate followers. In this manner, I was able to collect fairly detailed life histories from them and also observe their style of life and cult and noncult activities. Male members of the group were fewer in number, and they were also more difficult to interview since most were employed during the day and would only come to the feasts during the evenings.

The most difficult part of this first phase of fieldwork had to do with the traveling nature of cult activity. I thought at first that I would move in with Tanti, but as she was engaged in moving from group to group, this would have been fruitless. I had no alternative, therefore, but to base myself at a boarding house in the capital city and simply move with the group whenever a ceremony was held. While this was somewhat inconvenient and unsettling, the nature of the cult activity left me no other choice. However, it was also rewarding to be able to return to a degree of material comfort now and then, and it provided a good opportunity to rewrite notes and take stock of my data. By the middle of the field period, and after I had witnessed a numbers of feasts, I became interested in the medical and healing practices of the cult. The senior leader of the group was renowned for his healing and therapeutic skills, and I asked if I might live with him in his village in order to learn something about his work. He agreed to this and fortunately had another house near his own. I moved into it and engaged his sister-in-law as a cook. She proved to be a lively and articulate woman who made an excellent key informant. Shango leaders usually engage in healing and divination. The Shango king was particularly famous for these skills and had amassed a large clientele, both people from his immediate area and those who traveled to his village from all parts of the island seeking medical and psychological advice. By living in his house, I was able not only to converse with him regularly but also to observe his relationship with his "patients," the kinds of problems they brought to him, and the nature of the advice and/or medication which he supplied. On his busy consulting days as many as fifteen to twenty people would be gathered on his porch waiting, and I used this opportunity to meet and informally interview as many as possible and, in this manner, collected data on local beliefs in regard to physical and psychological illness, its symptoms, etiology, and methods of treatment.

In all, I spent six months in Trinidad, dividing my time between attending Shango feasts and gathering an interview sample of approximately forty leaders and their most active followers and living in the main leader's village.[2] No serious fieldwork problems were encountered, mainly because of the nature of my research problem and the kind of interest and cooperation it aroused among these strongly religious people.

II

During this period, Trinidad was beginning its drive toward political autonomy and nationalistic feelings were beginning to be aroused. In 1956, a newly formed nationalist party won the elections and assumed political power, thereby ousting the old colonial regime. Two years later saw the formation of the now defunct West Indies Federation, and in 1962 Trinidad became an independent country. As these political changes took place, and as the population gradually became politicized and deeply involved in political actions and sentiments, my own research interests changed in a similar manner. I returned early in 1965 to do a study broadly in the area of political development, but focusing specifically on the process of political commitment. The study had to do with the extent of political information people have, where they get it from (mass media, political rallies, and the like), the extent of their political participation, and their general attitudes toward the political system and its political role encumbents. While a study of this kind can presumably be done in a village or another centralized context using traditional anthropological techniques, it lends itself more readily to a survey research design in which a larger and more representative sample can be attained. In fact, research topics which have to do with development and modernization and which are of interest to a growing number of anthropologists call for increased sophistication of research techniques and methodology. Anthropologists conducting research within the context of emerging nations work on such topics as national integration, the rise of political consciousness among

---

[2] I returned to Trinidad two years later, and also spent some time in Grenada gathering comparative material on Shango there.

rural or peasant peoples, the changing structure of urban areas as a result of migration from rural areas, and many other sociopolitical problems which emerge from the development process. It becomes apparent that reliance on participant observation and other traditional techniques of anthropology cannot adequately cope with topics which involve the study of large segments of a population or indeed of entire nations (Leach 1967:75–89; Speckmann 1967:56–74).

The sample survey devised and used primarily by sociologists can be of immense value in gathering data on problems associated with a national state or any problem in which a representative sample of a large population is required. Some anthropologists have already successfully used the survey technique, and political scientists, particularly those at work in developing areas, are also making use of this instrument (Mitchell 1965:665–685; Almond and Verba 1965). The survey technique is not without its problems, however. These problems frequently have to do with mechanical procedures such as sample selection, questionnaire construction, and the like, and are thus very different to the kinds of problems the anthropological fieldworker experiences in the course of research. Before commenting on these, however, a word about the general research design is in order.

This research experience began very differently from my first study in that a research design was constructed before arrival in the field. In using the survey technique, and with the help of seven local interviewers, I was able to collect a total of 350 interviews. The sample was selected by means of the Trinidad and Tobago Census of 1960, which was conveniently divided into enumeration districts. The districts varied somewhat in size, although the average was about one-hundred households. Twenty districts were selected by using a table of random numbers. A questionnaire of 182 items was constructed before fieldwork began, and this was pretested in Trinidad and revised accordingly. Each district was surveyed and a number of streets or roads (in country areas) were randomly selected. The interviewers were then sent to these areas and instructed to approach each second house on the selected streets or roads until the total quota of interviews (usually fifteen to twenty-five, depending on the total size of the district) was reached.

While it is important to begin a study of this type with a prestructured research design, it must be stressed that the over-all research design—and particularly the sampling procedure—should be sufficiently flexible to permit changes in the field. This is especially necessary because field conditions in many areas of the world may not lend themselves to a rigid strategy of research. Bonilla, in making this point, also says that "what may appear in the abstract to be a clear-cut and vigorous plan can prove a nightmare to apply" (Bonilla 1964:145).

I selected my sample randomly because it would have been too difficult and time consuming to stratify the sample. Because of the availability of small census divisions, the random approach worked well in that a fairly representative sample of the country, on the basis of age, sex, race, and occupation was attained. Sampling units may, however, present another area of difficulty because the researcher must decide on the kinds of units to be used, and these may well depend on the country in which the research is to be carried out. Units can be villages, communities, neighborhood blocks, households, heads of households, and so forth. In countries which are not as developed as Trinidad, census units may not be available and even units such as households or roads may present problems of delineation (Wilson 1958:230–234). Even census divisions are not completely reliable due to the lapse of time between enumeration and the time of research. Changes in population or even in boundaries may seriously affect the sample. In this case, many enumeration districts were bounded by imaginary lines which were difficult to retrace so that some substitutions had to be made during the course of fieldwork. One district could not even be located during the first survey and rather than spending an excessive period of time locating the missing district, a substitution was made.

One of the advantages of the survey technique is that a large number of respondents can be reached. This usually means that a team of interviewers is employed to gather the data. One of the most obvious difficulties lies in finding trained local interviewers, since it is usually too expensive to bring an interview team into the field. In most countries, university students have some degree of of training, but they may not be available during the research period. (Summer research has an advantage in this respect.) Occasionally, a local market research or similar organization can supply reasonably well-trained interviewers. In Trinidad such facilities were fortunately available, but again several problems emerged. In the first instance, the natural biases of local interviewers had to be controlled. Since this study focused on politics, the interviewers themselves had strong opinions with respect to the political scene and a great deal of supervision was required to make sure that they were not leading or influencing the answers of the respondents. Even so, complete neutrality was probably not attained. Secondly, because of the racial heterogeneity in Trinidad, the interviewers and the respondents had to be matched with respect to race, insofar as this was possible. It was assumed, for example, that a Negro interviewer would not be able to establish sufficient rapport with an Indian respondent and vice versa. In other countries variables other than race—sex, for example—might have to be controlled (Ralis, Suchman, Golden 1958:245–250). Another problem is created by the fact that several interviewers are employed and inconsistencies or differences between them may affect the over-all results. Interviewer reliability may be increased by careful and prolonged training, but often the exigencies of fieldwork do not allow for such extensive training periods. I spent one week in familiarizing the interviewers with the study and the questionnaire. Part of the time was spent on interview techniques and role play among ourselves and with respondents. Each interviewer did five sample interviews before going into the field.

One of the major weaknesses of the survey technique is that it relies upon the voluntary cooperation of the respondents. However, this is not an insurmountable barrier, particularly as respondents can be substituted as long as substitutions are made in keeping with the research design. In a limited field situation, however, such substitutions may not be feasible and may, in fact, become excessively time consuming. Usually the interviewer is instructed to convince the respondent of the importance of the research in order to enlist his cooperation. Even so, this aspect of the survey technique may be most foreign to the anthropologist accustomed to the sometimes lengthy period of time necessary to establish rapport within a community. In this case, however, an interviewer went into an area in which he was not known and asked for one to two hours of a respondent's time. The interviewer is, of course, instructed to present his role and that of the research in a convincing and reasonable manner. Nevertheless, the time involved may be too short to really convince a potential respondent. Will people respond at all, and if they do, how valid are their responses? In this research project, again perhaps because it involved politics, many respondents tended to associate the interviewer with the government, despite assurances to the contrary. It could be seen that some respondents gave answers which they thought would not endanger them, and they were particularly loath to express any negative sentiment against the government. (These respondents tended to give vent to their true feelings after the formal interview was finished. For example, "You have no more questions, ma'am? Now the way I see it is this. . . .") Others tended to give the type of answers which they thought the interviewer expected. Some interesting rural-urban differences emerged in this respect. Urbanites tended to be far more suspicious; they asked many more questions, but tended to give fuller answers. Rural people, on the other hand, were more accepting but gave briefer answers and many more "I don't know" answers. (This may, of course, also reflect their lower level of information and political involvement.) Although rapport may present difficulties in some cases, the validity of the answers can, to some extent, be controlled by means of sensitive questionnaire construction.

Another problem which relates to the entire data-gathering process has to do with the need for government clearance of research in many areas of the world today. Government scrutiny may be necessary for many research projects regardless of the research design employed. Since the survey uses a questionnaire, the government official may wish to see the questionnaire and examine it carefully. There is a subtle psychological difference between showing a research proposal or discussing the research verbally and showing a questionnaire which lists a very specific set of questions. The chances are that an official will examine a questionnaire more closely and raise more objections when an itemized list is presented. The questionnaire used in this study was scrutinized carefully and changes were requested. Fortunately, they were not of a kind to seriously jeopardize the project—usually a rephrasing was sufficient. In other countries, major modifications might have to be made to satisfy a government official, and this is particularly the case when a questionnaire or other type of measuring instrument is employed.

Finally, the use of quantitative techniques such as the survey implies a problem of a somewhat different order. Many anthropologists are not trained in the sophisticated mechanics of questionnaire construction or statistical data analysis using computer programs. At the moment, this lack can be solved by reliance on sociological colleagues, but if quantitative techniques gain a more widespread acceptance among anthropologists, specific training, perhaps at the graduate level, may become necessary.

The survey design is thus a very different research procedure and it makes somewhat different demands on the researcher. While I surveyed all the districts chosen for the sample, trained the interviewers, and went along on each interview trip to supervise and check completed questionnaires (and conducted some interviews myself), my involvement was not as intense and personal relationships with informants, so characteristic of anthropological fieldwork, was lacking. Since so much time is spent on the mechanical procedures of data collection and the researcher only spends a few hours with each informant, the researcher becomes involved in procedures rather than people. This carries through to the data analysis phase where the quantitative data are coded, punched onto IBM cards, and analyzed through the computer. This differs markedly from the intense assembling, rewriting, and reordering of the anthropologist's field notes from which the major points of analysis gradually develop and emerge. Despite the various problems that may be encountered in using the survey in a field setting, this and other methodological techniques are useful to anthropology, particularly when combined with the more intensive field techniques which living in a community makes possible.

III

I turn now to the third study which, in terms of methodology, combined features of the two already discussed but which also presented a new set of problems. While studying the lower-class political commitment, I was also interested in finding out how the economic and political elites in this country felt about the various changes which had taken place; how they perceived the role of government in a newly independent country; and how, specifically, they viewed the interacting relationship between government, management, and labor. The latter problem was of particular importance because Trinidad, as many other developing countries, was then in the throes of labor unrest, and this situation, combined with other factors, had created an unusually tense political climate. The first phase of this study again consisted of isolating an adequate sample of political and economic elites. Since I had been following current events by subscribing to newspapers and maintaining contact with various individuals in Trinidad, I had a good idea of who the major elites were even before arrival in the country. The names of union leaders were readily available through the trade union register, and leading members of government and opposition parties were also easily identifiable. Top-level management officials were somewhat more difficult to locate, but this was done by interviewing three such individuals and asking them for the names of other leading company officials. My sample consisted of ten union leaders, fifteen senior members of government (including the Prime Minister), members of opposition parties, and seven management officials. The sample was by no means representative, nor did it tap all levels of the elite community, but consisted of individuals whom I could contact in the time available and who agreed to be interviewed. Randomness did not appear to be as important a criterion to selection as did the qualities and beliefs of individuals themselves. I sought those union leaders who were, for example, articulate and who were known to hold very strong opinions and views on various issues.

In terms of procedure, I would either phone the respondent and briefly explain my purpose to him (or, more usually to his secretary) and request permission for an interview, or visit his office and make an appointment personally. In making this first contact and at the time of the interview, I would present my university credentials and briefly explain the purpose of my study on political commitment and the need to complement this study with the views of the elite community. I had with me a copy of the questionnaire from that study, and a general discussion of it usually paved the way to the interview itself. These interviews were unstructured, although I had six or seven questions in mind which were asked of each respondent. Generally, however, the respondent guided the interview and I would merely interject questions at particularly relevant points. Many respondents were quite cooperative and talked freely, whereas some simply answered a question and would await the next one. I generally asked permission to record notes, and this was given in all cases; seven interviews were tape recorded. Some of the respondents were already known to me and the interview in these cases usually took place under informal conditions and was conducted along conversational lines. With a few, the rapport between respondent and interviewer was especially close and subsequent informal meetings followed.

Finding the sample and gaining access to the respondents did not present undue difficulties, in part because of my prior familiarity with this society and its elite community. (In many of the smaller developing countries, the elite community is in itself small and highly visible and, with proper credentials and contacts, is usually accessible to a foreign investigator.) This type of study does, however, add another dimension to the fieldwork process.

In terms of practical problems, one must first contend with the fact that elites are generally urban based and this involves the researcher with difficulties that may be created by an urban research environment. By way of contrast, the researcher is rarely able to live within the elite community because it is usually to be found in upper-class residential neighborhoods where temporary housing is generally unavailable. Another alternative is to live in the city and meet informants in their offices or occasionally at their homes. As much or more time is spent in traveling to and from an appointment as in the interview itself. In most studies which emphasize interview techniques, the researcher is dependent upon the cooperation of the informant, and this is especially important in a study of elites. These individuals are generally occupied with time-consuming activities, and frequently an interview appointment must be made weeks in advance. An interviewer may not be given more than a short period of time—in some cases as little as half an hour. Ideally, a researcher tries to fill up his available days so that at least two interviews can be conducted in a day. Frequently this kind of schedule is impossible to maintain so that days may go by without a single interview. I found on some occasions that after having made an appointment with an individual weeks in advance, I would arrive at the appointed time only to be told by a secretary that some urgent business had made the informant unavailable. Members of the elite may also frequently be out of the country or involved in meetings and tours within the country and thus inaccessible for long periods of time. In view of these many and varied demands on their time, collecting even a relatively small sample of elite respondents may in the long run be exceedingly time consuming for the researcher. While my total sample consisted of only thirty-two respondents, the interviews took two months to collect. Part of my time, however, was occupied with attendance at political meetings, sittings of the House of Representatives, and the like.

In addition to these practical problems, there are others relating to the actual relationship between interviewer and respondent. Anthropological fieldworkers in the course of their research usually interact with informants who are relatively unsophisticated, uneducated, poor, and in general of lower status than the fieldworker. Although many fieldworkers deliberately attempt to establish an egalitarian relationship with their informants, the fact of their being foreign, thought to be rich and powerful, and usually members of the white race almost automatically places them in a superior position vis-à-vis the informant. In a study of elites however, the relationship between the two is one of relative equality and, in many cases, in fact, the roles may be reversed. While a foreign, white professor may have high status, he is nevertheless interacting with individuals who may own, control, or be part of a vast financial empire or who may, by virtue of political office, have a high degree of political power and be on close terms with leading international political figures. For example, at the beginning of an interview with a cabinet minister, he mentioned that he had recently been a dinner guest of the Canadian Prime Minister, whom he thought to be a "charming man." I could merely nod politely, not ever having experienced this honor myself. In addition to their economic and political power, elites are generally foreign trained, university educated, and of a high level of cultural sophistication. The social distance between researcher and informant is thus greatly minimized, and the need for a totally different orientation to the interview situation becomes necessary. The interviewer must present himself and the research problem in far more detail. He must expect to be questioned at some length about himself, his own background, his reasons for coming to this particular country, the rationale behind his selection of informants, and a wide variety of other topics. He will also be called upon to provide information regarding his own personal attitudes. In other words, in interviewing elites, a researcher cannot expect to merely ask questions and await replies —he is called upon to participate and, in fact, be interviewed himself. The demeanor of the interviewer must sometimes be one of deference and almost humility, particularly with senior-level government officials. The interviewer often has not had the opportunity to interact with or study elite members of his own society so that this may often be his first experience in interacting with powerful individuals. While prior research experience is, of course, an advantage, in that research and particularly interview skills are cumulative, one may, nevertheless, become somewhat apprehensive in these situations.

The researcher may also be put under stress in cases where an informant wishes not only to discuss the particular research study but also to question the nature of the economic and political commitments of the researcher. In the past, fieldworkers involved in the more traditional research situations of anthropology were frequently asked to state their views and personal values in regard to religion, kinship, and similar concerns, and this is still the case when working on such topics with rural or less-sophisticated informants. When anthropologists work on the modernizing sectors of the community in which some interaction—if not a detailed study—of economic and political elites is maximized, personal views in regard to policy and ideological commitments will be asked for. This is particularly the case when the researcher is North American, and he may be asked his views in regard to the foreign (and domestic) policy commitments of the United States. The resulting strain on a researcher is thus formidable—he may be asked to defend and/or criticize the policies of his own country. When researchers are questioned about the sources of their funds and when they are, in fact, government supported, this difficulty may be enhanced (Beals 1967). In my experience, my own views on current international politics and the role of Canada and the United States in particular were frequently questioned, especially by politicians. Similarly, my opinions would be solicited in regard to the political and economic situation in Trinidad. A particularly difficult situation developed in the course of this study because of the conflict between government and the trade unions. Union leaders wanted to know where I stood in regard to the role of labor in general and on the Trinidad conflict in particular. Some attempted to pressure me to agree with their side of the issue, and in a few cases it was made quite clear that unless I stated my ideological position in terms agreeable to the respondent, the interview would be terminated. The issue came to a head with reference to a specific piece of labor legislation enacted during my field period. Union officials denounced it vehemently and expected that I would also react negatively to the legislation, whereas some government officials went to great lengths to convince me of its necessity and desirability. This raises an important issue in regard to research procedure. Some researchers maintain that a researcher can use any reasonable means in the interests of gathering data, whereas others feel that some moral constraints must be operative in setting limits. I attempted to maintain a neutral position or tried to hide behind the cloak of ignorance. During some interviews, however, this procedure did not work and I was forced to indicate some degree of agreement or at least sympathy with a particular point of view. Where issues have factionalized the community, researchers may be caught between and manipulated by the respondents, usually to the disadvantage of the researcher and his needs. Whatever moral position a researcher espouses, it seems apparent that in studies of the impact of modernization where interaction with an elite population may be crucial, some degree of commitment on the part of the researcher is essential (Henry 1966:552–559).

I have outlined in brief the research strategy used in three studies undertaken in the same country by the same investigator over a time span of eight years. In terms of comparison, these studies differ in their theoretical aims, in the methods employed to gather the data, and in the sample of informants used. In the study of the Shango cult, a fairly traditional approach to a problem of long-standing interest to anthropology was taken. The general aim of the project was to describe the religious practices of the cult and to analyze the social and psychological dynamics of behavior within the group. Participant observation and unstructured interviewing were the major tools, and the sample consisted of a relatively unsophisticated lower-class population. Aside from the initial difficulty in locating the group and the inconvenience involved in frequent traveling, very few problems emerged during the fieldwork. The study of political commitment also concentrated on lower-class informants, but the research procedure differed markedly in that the survey technique was used to obtain a larger sample of informants. The structured interview, using a questionnaire, was the major data-gathering tool, and most of the interviews were conducted by local interviewers. In addition to the various technical difficulties that confront any survey researcher, a number of other problems emerged from this study. Even in a relatively open country such as Trinidad, where research efforts are still welcomed, I felt that a study of political development called for government clearance of the project. While several changes in the questionnaire were required, these were relatively minor and did not interfere with the aims of the study. In many other countries, however, far greater restrictions may be placed on the researcher, and, in fact, research efforts which deal with sensitive areas may not be undertaken. For the anthropologist engaged in survey research on whatever topic, however, perhaps one of the greatest problems arises from the psychological reorientation necessary for a structured study which does not involve the long period of fieldwork characteristic of anthropological research.

The third study also used informal interviewing as in the Shango study, but differed most in that the social distance between researcher and elite informants was minimized and therefore called for a new set of role relations between the two. Because it dealt with the problems of modernization for political and economic elites, it brought into sharp focus the need of the researcher to formally communicate his personal and ideological commitment to the informant.

In summary, my own feeling is that all methodological procedures present their particular difficulties to a fieldworker. While a few standardized formulas for the success of a fieldwork project exist (the do's and don'ts of fieldwork), in the final analysis, the skills and experience of each researcher in relation to the situation in which he undertakes to work seem to be the more crucial factors. The success of fieldwork is largely the result of the unique interaction between the personality of the fieldworker, the nature of the research problem, and the socio-cultural environment in which research is undertaken.

4

Rapport and Resistance among the Embu of Central Kenya (1963-1964)

SATISH SABERWAL

THE ROAD FROM Nairobi passes through Embu Township (population about 5500) on its way around Mount Kenya to Meru. For about 20 miles before reaching Embu, the old road, still used in 1963, winds in hairpin bends around the foothills of Mount Kenya. Eighty miles from Nairobi, Embu is tucked away in the folds of the mountain, far from Kenya's great tourist routes, little noticed by the world, or even by Kenya until the recent spurt in coffee production. The Embu streams have superb trout, however, and the Izaac Walton Inn uses the news dailies of Nairobi to beacon its residents to the trout and to the Inn's splendid cuisine, well-stocked bar, and comfortable rooms. Late in January 1963 Derrick Stenning, then the Director of the East African Institute of Social Research, escorted me to Embu Township; we called at the office of the District Commissioner, looking for a place where I could live, observe and work.[1]

The District Commissioner was out, but his assistant, the District Officer I, a young Briton, received us. With Derrick watching benignly, I explained that I wished to spend a year, possibly a little longer, doing fieldwork in his district. He pointed to the 1 : 50,000 maps covering his office wall and asked me to choose where I wished to go. After some discussion I decided that I would work in Embu Division, where the people called the Embu lived (see map), and where the prospects of finding a house for my wife, our three-month-old daughter, and myself were

[1] Credit for supporting the fieldwork from January 1963 to June 1964 goes to the Foreign Area Fellowship Program of the Joint Committee of the Social Science Research Council and the American Council of Learned Societies; this paper was written while I was a Research Associate of McGill's Centre for Developing-Area Studies and was aided by McGill's Social Sciences Committee on Research. Stanley Freed, Regula Qureshi, Edith Saberwal, and fellow contributors to this volume criticized an earlier draft, but the responsibility for the present version is mine.

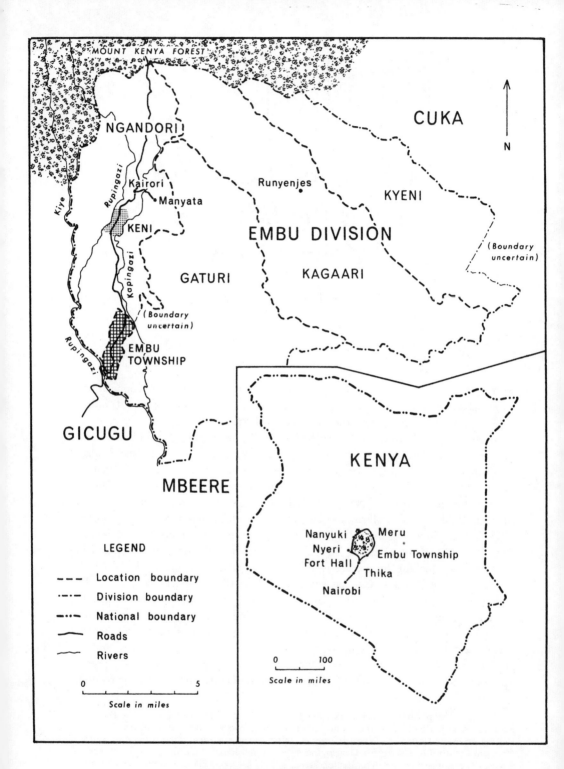

EMBU DIVISION

good. Two government stone houses were vacant in the area, and I would be permitted to rent government furniture also. He promised to tell the District Officer of the Embu Division, who lived in Runyenjes, about me on the wireless the next morning: This gentlemen would show me the houses and introduce me to the chief in the area. The District Officer I later asked Derrick and me to lunch, and we were glad of a good day's work done.

A couple of days later the District Officer took me around his division and showed me the houses. In one of them the water supply was problematical, and, besides, a government survey was being conducted in its neighborhood at the time; it would be better to take the other one. We met the chief, a young man in his midthirties who spoke excellent English, drove a Ford Anglia, and had recently taken the football team from his location to Nairobi to play against the Embu residents in Nairobi; his team had lost. During the next week my wife and I visited Embu two or three times, arranging housecleaning, water supply, and an interpreter, and taking our supplies into the house. At 5000 feet in altitude in the early February summer days, we drove through crisp air along the slowly climbing ridges which shouldered the fresh, recently built, dispersed homes and some dilapidated, nucleated villages. Close to our new house were the chief's office, the houses of several tribal policemen, a dispensary, and the pharmacist's house, and a number of other huts in varying stages of disrepair: Perhaps this would be the local community I would study, but I was uncertain.

We had arrived in Kenya nearly six weeks earlier, and had done some traveling in connection with a conference sponsored by the East African Institute of Social Research. Kenya would be independent within a year, and the imminent political changes made the immigrants (Asians and Europeans) feel insecure and afraid for the future. They had only limited personal contacts with Africans, and the harsh memories of the Mau Mau uprising (peak: 1952–1956) remained. Some of them told us the precautions that we ought to take in our dealings with Africans; for example, we should not pick up hitchhikers, especially at night. Of course, we ignored the stereotypes and the prescribed social distance. During the initial weeks our contacts in Embuland were very cordial and entirely free from unpleasant incident, which seemed surprising for an area which had recently emerged from the Mau Mau Emergency, but we were not inclined then to question the bases of our good fortune.

For about a month, uncertain about the "local community" I would focus on, I "played for time" by talking with the subchief in my area, a friendly government official, about kin terms, kin behavior, marriage, land tenure, and whatever else caught my interest. Within the previous five years, the Embu had undergone "Land Consolidation" leading to a major redistribution of land rights: in the Land Office in Embu Township I was able to locate not only detailed records of the litigation during the Land Consolidation but also new 1 : 2500 maps showing every field in the area: I arranged to get copies of these maps. A large coffee cooperative was brought to my attention, and I visited its office and briefly surveyed its records. The members of an elders' council, constituted to hear disputes by the chief, were commended to me as repositories of traditional knowledge; I visited the council's meetings and inquired whether I could be made an elder. I visited the nearby teachers' training college and heard about the process of its growth. I walked around, exploring the hills and the valleys, shaking hands, and talking with whoever cared to ask me what I was doing. One month after moving into the house initially, I decided that the Embu in 1963 had no local communities continuous with the precolonial residential patterns: The disruption during the Mau Mau Emergency and the subsequent Land Consolidation had scrambled the population; nor would a village be a convenient focus for observation, for village residents were in the process of leaving their villages and moving into the fields to which they had recently acquired title—the village communities were disintegrating. Within his sublocation, however, the subchief saw seven "blocks" of fields, and I sought his help in locating a block where one of its residents would rent me a room or build me a small hut. When a man, to be called John,[2] agreed to build the hut, his block of about 200 acres, containing about two-hundred persons and delimited rather arbitrarily by the subchief, became my unit for intensive observation; it was called Keni.

Within a week or so of deciding to concentrate on Keni, I visited, with my wife and child, nearly every homestead in it; we introduced ourselves, explaining what I was doing, and chatting generally. During the next few weeks I began census interviews with the heads of families in each homestead: I sought information on names, age, education, occupational history, hut type, parentage, and pattern of interaction with kinsmen. Some families were frank and reliable from the first visit. In others one member was reliable and another was not. Yet others were cautious or hostile in the beginning and became friendlier later. The following case concerns such a transformation:

Case 1: It was about a month after deciding to focus on Keni that I first met Njage. My census and other interviews with others in the neighborhood had been going well; Njage's homestead was rather out of the way, and during two or three earlier visits there I had not met him. On April 24 he was working on his coffee trees and indicated that he would talk with me the next day. During the next two days I visited his homestead three times, and he was out every time. A week later I met him lounging in his cousin's homestead, where several people were busy making beer. To raise the matter of interviews in this setting appeared to be inappropriate.

May 5. I went to the beer party at Njage's cousin's homestead and stayed there for about an hour. One normally bought beer at these parties and shared it with others present. In this case the host "bought" a panful of beer for me. I took a little, and then Njage emptied the pan. Then I "bought" a half-shilling worth, and he drank most of that also. A little drunk now, he led the following conversation with me:

He said that he had deliberately absented himself from appointments with me because he didn't know why I wanted to ask all those questions. As an aside he said that he would answer my questions if I would help him pay the bridewealth for a second wife: His present wife already had four children, and if he

---

[2] To protect identities, all Embu names in this paper are fictitious.

continued with her, he could have many more—maybe nine; so he wanted my help in getting a second wife. I explained briefly that I really didn't have the resources to pay bridewealth.

Njage wanted me to drink beer, and two or three times he insisted on my drinking from the glass he had already used. I said that doctors thought this was unhygienic, but if he insisted, I would drink beer from his glass. There was a moment of tense expectation in the group, and they were a little startled when I did drink from his glass. Then he said that I need not fear him and could ask him anything.

At one point he laid his arm next to mine and said, "If I kill you, will you then say that you are black or brown?" When I replied that most people when killed don't say anything, everyone laughed and I had to shake hands around the circle.

Later, as I was leaving the group, he insisted on my staying and buying more beer for him if I wished to talk with him later. Saying that I had run out of money and that I had to go and see other people, I left; he was clearly unhappy at my departure.

May 7. At the beer party Njage had offered to see me today. When I arrived, he was weeding his plot of sweet potatoes. I did a little weeding with him. He had a visitor from another neighborhood today, and he said he would see me tomorrow afternoon.

May 8. Went to his homestead twice this afternoon. His daughter said that he went away in the morning, she didn't know where.

May 16. Njage was not home, and his wife said she didn't know where he was.

May 23. Njage was not home.

May 24. Saw Njage, he made an appointment for May 29.

May 29. Njage was not home; his wife said he had gone to work in someone else's coffee field.

May 30. I visited Kori, who lives several fields away from Njage. Kori asked me in to drink beer. During conversation Kori said that Njage had told him that he wasn't going to talk with me because he didn't know what I wanted from them. He also asked Kori not to talk with me. While we were drinking, Njage passed by and I hailed him. I said that we looked for him yesterday; he said he had asked us to come the day before and not yesterday—my interpreter assured him that he was in error. I said that I could only ask him to talk with me as one man to another; if he didn't want to talk with me, I could not force him because I was not a government man. He did not comment. He drank a couple of mugs of beer, but Kori kept me engaged in other conversation.

June 9. Mbogo had promised to talk with me tonight, and my interpreter and I were walking with him to my hut in the neighborhood when we met Njage and two of Mbogo's brothers singing along the road; the three men, mildly drunk, were in high spirits. Njage pulled me to a side, and we sat on the road bank talking. As usual when Njage was drunk, the discussion was a context wherein he tried to come to terms with me and I encouraged him to do this. He said that he had finally discovered that I was a robber like himself; in reply I said very good, would he form a company with me so we could go rob someone; he didn't reply. Again, he asked what my parents would think if he killed me then; I said, don't worry, they'll never find out, go ahead and kill me. This kind of banter continued for about fifteen minutes. It was very dark. Two or three cars came by and had to avoid running over Mbogo's brothers, who were engaged in horseplay on the road. Njage went off to talk to the woman in whose land my hut was. Later, as I was doing Mbogo's census, Njage came to my hut, took a chair, and interrupted us several times. Every time I impressed on him my need to continue with Mbogo; every time he said okay, keep going, then interrupted a few minutes later. After about an hour I announced that it was time we all went home. Njage said that he would like me to go to see him early tomorrow morning, even though I would have to break my date with Gacai.

June 10. After talking with Gacai, I went to Njage's homestead in mid-morning. His wife said that he had just gone off.

June 11. Njage's wife said he was working in his field halfway down the hill. We went down to where he was working. I asked if he would like to do the census. He agreed and we had a very pleasant interview. His previous hostility seemed to be all gone. To my question of why he had been so evasive before, he said they had just not understood what I was doing.

During the months that followed, Njage became one of my steady, reliable informants in the neighborhood. He did not ever try to mislead me.

It was after more than fifteen visits to his homestead and three encounters elsewhere that I was able to begin interviewing him.[3] In some cases, as in the following, sheer persistence was a tactic of no value.

Case 2: Fragmentary biographical data indicate that Ireri had had an unhappy childhood. Later on, two of his five wives had died, a third (whose mention infuriated him) had left him, and the other two lived in his homestead. Ireri was a morose old man who spent most of his time with his small herd of livestock. After days of cajoling I would get him into an interview situation, and twenty minutes later he would leave, announcing that he absolutely had to attend to his cattle. Furthermore, he refused to talk about his family and children: shortly after the recent government census enumeration one of his children had died, and he was not going to talk about his children again. After several tries it became clear that I would never get very far with Ireri.

So I turned my attention to Ireri's two wives and his eldest son living with him. The son was willing but not very well informed. The wives were cordial and answered specific questions about names, age, education, and so forth, but I always had to compete with five or six children around the house demanding their attention, and usually the children won. In April 1964, nearly a year after I started, I was still adding bits of information to this family's census. Then, late in May, Ireri's senior wife came to our house and asked me to take her to fetch her married

---

[3] None of these visits took more than a few minutes each. I visited his homestead whenever I was in the area visiting other families.

daughter from the hospital fifteen miles away. I was very glad to oblige. I went through my notebooks, summarized my information on the family in code, and put this summary on the dashboard of the car along with my census schedule. As I drove her to the hospital and back at slow speed, I asked her all the questions about her family and had the interpreter write down her answers. Her daughter too contributed to the information. The census was completed.

Dame Fortune sent Ireri's wife my way, and I seized the opportunity. A fieldworker has to be just as alert to the threat of loss of good informants. The next three cases illustrate the kinds of efforts continually necessary to maintain one's social relations in the community.

Case 3: Robert was one of my prize informants. In his late sixties, he knew a great deal about Embu traditions, and was willing to talk with me about them for an hour or two at a time, day after day. By late 1963 he had talked with me for some fifty hours. Until then nearly every interview had indicated new directions for inquiry, and Robert had talked willingly. Then, in November, the stream began to dry up. Robert would answer a query briefly and terminate the interview fairly quickly. Something had gone wrong, but I couldn't tell what. Meanwhile, I had several other projects on hand and I was willing to let Robert rest.

When in mid-February his son Simon brought a bride to Robert's homestead, I took a gift of 5 pounds of sugar and ten shillings to the homestead, and gave these to Robert's wife and Simon's bride, who were working in a field together. Simon was away, but Robert was weeding another field. I walked over to Robert. He kept on working, and stopped to shake hands with me after a long while. I took over his fork and did some digging. I said that I wanted to talk with him about his son's marriage, and he inquired curtly why I was so interested in marriages. Marriages are important in life, I said, and I wished to compare his son's marriage with his own which he had described to me earlier. Robert continued to be somewhat hostile for a while, then he told me why he was angry with me.

Traditionally, the Embu have attached great importance to a ceremony for adolescent girls during which their clitoris would be removed. During the colonial period, both the British administration and the Anglican missionaries repeatedly conducted crusades against the clitoridectomy operation, and most Embu stuck just as tenaciously to the traditional practice. There is, however, an Anglican minority among the Embu many of whose members do not have their daughters operated on and who prefer to marry unoperated girls. Back in October I had discussed the matter with Robert, who condemned the Anglican position very strongly; I had asked him how he would react if his son were to wish to marry an Anglican girl who had not been operated; Robert had replied that his son could marry her only when Robert was dead.

Soon after this conversation the Embu court served Simon with a summons charging him with having impregnated a girl. Premarital pregnancies in Embuland are fairly common and reflect the permissive Embu view of premarital sex. However, in this case, the girl happened to be an Anglican—and unclitoridectomized. The coincidence upset Robert deeply: He decided that either I had known about the case beforehand or had told the girl's family about his attitude to such a marriage. He was offended at the thought that I had acted as a spy against him.

The girl in question lived several miles away, and I knew neither her nor any of her kinsmen. It took me half an hour of patient argument to convince Robert that the course of events was entirely explicable without my telling anyone what his views were: The girl would tell her father that Simon was the genitor, her father had probably seen her in Simon's company, and since Simon didn't want to marry her, her father would sue him for compensation. Robert accepted my innocence. We arranged to go to the Catholic service together next Sunday. Later we resumed our interviews; in all I talked with him for nearly two-hundred hours.

In this case I could not possibly have anticipated the misunderstanding. The next two cases concern situations where, anticipating the damaging consequences of my actions, I moved to take remedial actions.

Case 4: When in December 1963 I found it necessary to dismiss Paul, one of my two interpreters, on strong suspicion of repeated thefts, I had to move to protect my relationship with his wife's father's brother, John; my hut in Keni was located in his homestead, and besides he was a very good friend and informant.

Several years before becoming my interpreter Paul had been the headmaster of a primary school. He had lost the job because he had embezzled several thousand shillings of school money. I learned about this a few weeks before my decision to dismiss him. When I explained my decision to John, he said that he had been surprised when I had taken Paul initially; he had not warned me against hiring Paul because even evil men can change over time. Insofar as Paul spent most of his earnings over beer and women, John said that his dismissal would not affect his wife and children adversely: John's family took care of them.

The next case, also involving a theft, was considerably more complex.

Case 5: On the morning of October 5, my interpreter Moses bought a new shirt in Embu township, and it was lying unopened in my car that afternoon when we parked the car in Keni and went to visit in the neighborhood. When we returned, we found that the car, which had almost certainly been locked, had been broken into, and Moses' shirt and a torchlight stolen.

Several months earlier someone had broken into my hut in John's homestead and had stolen my rainboots. To recover the cost from my insurance company, I had registered that theft with the police then; the police had done nothing about it, but the insurance company had compensated me. This time Moses went to the police station and registered the theft of his shirt from my car.

Oct. 16. As Moses and I were walking through Keni, a group of four or five boys stopped us and told Moses that Ben, a boy who lived just south of Keni, had stolen the shirt and that it had been hidden somewhere. With this information from Moses, two policemen went to Keni and took Ben and three other boys to the police station. The boys told the police then that the shirt was hidden in the house of Maculus, a good friend of mine; the police took the shirt from Maculus' house and the torch from the home of one of the boys. Upon hearing of this, I went to the police station, saw the two items, and learned that the police intended to keep the boys there overnight.

Then I drove to Maculus' house and also visited Munyi, the father of one of the arrested boys who lived in Keni. Both the men said that Munyi's son had found the shirt in the bush and had given it to Maculus' wife, so she would turn it over to me; since I had not visited her homestead for several days, she had not had an opportunity to give me the shirt.

Oct. 17. The police presented the boys to court and accused Maculus' wife of sheltering stolen things.

Oct. 19. The court called the parents of each boy and asked them whether they were training their children properly. The parents were also warned that they would be fined if their children were caught stealing again. Maculus' wife was found guilty of sheltering stolen things and fined thirty shillings. Moses went to the hearing and identified the things. I decided to stay away.

When I visited Maculus' house later, his wife, close to tears, said that she could not understand why we had brought in the police. Others in her homestead were equally bewildered. I saw that I could save my relationship with this family only by accepting responsibility for their discomfort. I said that it was my fault that I had let Moses register the theft with the police; instead, I should have sought the help of my friends in that neighborhood. Therefore, I offered to pay the thirty shillings in fine. Maculus and his wife accepted the offer.

Oct. 23. We heard a rumor that Munyi had let his neighbors know that he would sue Moses for trespass if Moses entered Munyi's fields again. With my other interpreter I went to Munyi. He was cordial and said that he had nothing against me. The fault was Moses' for he had gone to the police precipitately, and this had led to his son getting almost imprisoned; therefore the parents of the boys who had been taken to the police station had resolved not to let Moses enter their fields or to talk to me through him. I suggested to Munyi that Moses' error had been due to his youth and inexperience and urged consideration and forgiveness upon him. Munyi was adamant and demanded an apology from Moses. Initially Moses was reluctant to apologize to Munyi, for he felt his position to be righteous, but he agreed to go to Munyi when I pointed out that his usefulness to me depended upon his being acceptable to Munyi and other residents in Keni.

My final case concerns a situation where I had to help my wife out of trouble.

Case 6: About half way through my fieldwork, one day I returned home to find our house surrounded by a mob of boys in school uniforms. They were peering into the house through the glass windows. I asked them what they wanted. They said, "Water." I went inside and found my wife in disarray. The boys, visiting the dispensary in a group for a medical check had heard about the strange foreigners living in this house and had walked over. Our neighbors, who had always been welcome inside, had never felt the need to peer through the windows.

Initially the boys had tried to get water from a tank behind our house, but it was empty. They started looking through the windows, and my wife went outside. Many of them were standing in front of the house. They asked her for water, and she said that she did not have water (which we boiled for drinking) for so many people; for a while she sat on the porch. Then she returned inside, and the boys converged on the windows. She did the first thing that came to her mind: she started making faces at them! The boys thought this was great fun, and their numbers grew. She felt helpless and was distraught by the time I arrived.

I had no interpreter available then. Within the limits of their knowledge of English and my knowledge of Kiembu, I told the boys that we did not have drinking water for so many people; would they please get the water somewhere else. Some of them went away, but many lingered. It was clear that I could not influence them directly. Therefore, I walked over to the chief's office, about three-hundred yards away around a couple of corners. I hoped to find there some Embu friend who would speak to the boys. I found the subchief, who had helped me ever since I had begun living there. I explained the situation briefly. He walked over to our house, asked the boys where the teacher escorting them was, admonished them for misbehaving, told them where they could get water, and asked them to leave. I think he also went over to the teacher and asked him to keep his pupils under control. We had no difficulty with the boys after that.

Discussion

I have presented here a selection of dyadic relationships involving me and my informants; the last case, an exception, was easily terminated. Needless to say, upon entering the field situation as a stranger, one has to develop a complex and extensive network of social relations rapidly. To maintain these relations in good repair requires a wide range of interpersonal sensitivity and response capacity. A fund of human sympathy is useful. It is also necessary to translate this sympathy into acts which your neighbors will recognize to be acts of goodwill. It takes some trial and error, but given the intent, one can usually find the form.

Like every anthropologist, my wife and I learned the local phrases for hello and farewell upon arrival and used these as appropriate. Over the 8-mile stretch from Embu Township to our home in Kairori, there were often people carrying loads to and from the market in the township. We used to pick up those going our way to our car's capacity. Since we lived next to the dispensary, patients too sick for the pharmacist's skills sometimes needed to go to the hospital in the township; we let it be known that we would provide an ambulance service for such cases. Women in labor often wished to go to the hospital, and we were summoned at all hours of day and night. This service was not limited to my informants; we responded to anyone in need who came to our home. Since this was a "universalistic" gesture, it generated fairly widespread acceptance, if not enthusiasm, for my research.

Yet, as these cases have shown, goodwill is not enough. Every community has its difficult individuals, and even the most sympathetic friend sometimes interprets one's actions in ways other than one can anticipate. Errors are often compounded, without one's knowing what is happening. These situations call for calm analysis. One must think through the rights and wrongs of the various actors involved, the sanctions available to each, the probability that these might be applied, and the extent of damage that could ensue. Sensitivity to others' discomfort is essential, though sometimes difficult to achieve in a cultural context one understands only partially.

There is the difficult man: He wants you to pay the bridewealth for his second wife; he drops in to visit you every evening though you know full well that he has nothing to tell you; he alleges that the beer party you organized was intended to get people drunk so that you could wrench their secrets from them. The unreasonable demand of the unreasonable individual is best met coolly and firmly: He is likely to be unreasonable with other people too, and they will often reject his allegations if you have previously projected an image of generalized goodwill. In resisting excessive demands, it is useful to enunciate general rules: We let it be known that we would take patients to hospital, but we would not transport wedding parties, politicians going to distant rallies, litigants going to the court, and the like.

We must also remember the element of time. What is seen to be based on ignorance in the first few months may be interpreted as an insult later on. As we understand the local cultural idiom better and enter personal relationships of greater depth, the danger that we might do the wrong thing increases; but as the case of Robert's son (Case 3) showed, our growing understanding of the cultural context should also increase our capacity to show that our actions were, in fact, harmless and acceptable.

While my relations with several organizations—the administration, the cooperatives, the churches, and the schools—were free and easy, the situation regarding the Kenya African National Union (KANU), the only political party in Embu Division, was different. I turn now to my relationship with KANU and its leaders.

Local politics was not a major focus of study for me when I went to Kenya. I had read brief references to the Embu in books written by a couple of administrators, but these concerned the precolonial society. I also knew a little about the upheaval attending the Mau Mau Emergency, but it was clearly inadequate for defining my research interests with precision ahead of the time. By and large, I had intended to let the nature of the contemporary society determine the directions of my inquiry. My field data for the first three months consist largely of kin terms, marriage types, land tenure, elders' council, census, and discussions with two old men concerning the institutions of the precolonial society. However, 1963 was the year in which Kenya was going to attain independence, and politics dominated Embu thought at this time; to choose to ignore political activity then was to condemn oneself to a study of the trivial. Yet the Embu perceived politics as the area whose "secrets" required protection from foreigners; they had accepted this task in the oaths which most of them had taken during the Mau Mau uprising. Everyone in the party felt bound to ignore and, when possible, frustrate my slowly growing interest in understanding contemporary political activity. I proceed now to discuss my tactics in this situation and to assess the extent of their effectiveness.

It is necessary to remember that none of the Keni residents appeared in any of the contemporary political leadership roles. Political activity was bounded more significantly by the administrative unit called a location, roughly fifty square miles in area with some twenty-thousand residents. Near its center, in a large market, Manyata, was the KANU locational office; in its vicinity I established my limited contacts with KANU leaders. The first Embu elections based on secret adult suffrage were due late in May. KANU announced its candidates in mid-March. One of them was opposed by an Independent.

On April 26 I went to an election rally in Manyata for the first time. I sat on the ground with the audience and watched the bugles, drums, songs, dances, slogans, speeches, and ululation (prolonged, shrill yells of appreciation), all of which made the party meetings in Embuland a stimulating experience. Some prominent people at the meeting permitted me to take pictures provided I promised to supply the KANU office with some enlargements. Three weeks later at another meeting, while I was taking pictures from a housetop, some members of the audience protested, but party leaders intervened to say that I had their permission. (Several months later, at a meeting in another area the audience protested again. The leaders' intervention failed to reassure the audience this time, and I had to discontinue taking pictures.) I asked my friends whom they intended to vote for and why; a few insisted that this was a private matter. I watched the polling and the victory celebrations later. In brief, the situations I observed were defined by the party to be open and public. I was beginning to identify some of the leaders and to frame some questions I would have liked answered. For the moment I didn't know who might answer them, but I was in no hurry; I had other projects going.

Working in low key proved to be beneficial in the long run. During these several months the local party leaders were presumably getting information about my activities and forming their own judgments concerning my true intentions. For example, as the typescript of my field notes came in from a typist in Nairobi, I regularly turned it over to one of my assistants for proofreading and cross-pagination. Whether the political leaders asked him about my notes, I do not know; but if they did, he would have been a source of reassurance. Furthermore, two KANU leaders had close relatives in Keni; one of them was also related to one of my interpreters. Another leader, a less influential man, lived next door to us and could keep us under surveillance.

Occasionally at rallies and elsewhere I would meet party leaders, but in various subtle ways they made it clear that they expected me to maintain a considerable distance from them. Meanwhile, my understanding of the situation grew slowly, indirectly. For example, at the end of July, KANU organized a council to nominate the party candidates for another set of elections, this time for two statutory local councils. My interpreter Paul (Case 4) wished to be a candidate and was interviewed by the council; from him I learned the nominating procedure in detail. Again, in October, through the elders' council mentioned earlier, I came into contact with a young woman who was having serious difficulties with her dead husband's kinsmen. She talked with me at great length about her difficulties, her fears of poisoning by the affinal kinsmen, and her visits to the medicine man to get protective treatment against this poison. She also happened to be an enthusiastic dancer at KANU rallies and often showed acute anxiety about the party's censure for talking with me. She told me that her colleagues had repeatedly warned her not to discuss politics with me. I did not learn anything about the content of politics from her, but the nature of boundary-maintaining mechanisms at work became slightly clearer.

In early November I began a series of lengthy interviews with Tai, an elder who had led his descent group in a famous land case about twenty years earlier. He talked to me about this and other cases and also about his relations with several close kinsmen. Since he was also a KANU leader, after several interviews I tried to steer the conversation to politics, but he avoided discussion by saying we would talk about it some other time.

At about the same time I told KANU leaders that I was interested in the Embu dispute-settlement procedures. My assistant had for several months maintained a journal of disputes coming to the elders' council sponsored by the chief. Since a KANU council also made itself available for listening to any disputes the litigants might bring to it, I sought permission to attend its meetings so that I might compare the approaches of the two councils. The leaders postponed a decision on my request from week to week, but I was allowed to address the council regarding my request: From its proceedings it became clear that the council was divided in its attitude to me, but it would allow me access to its meetings *only if its members agreed to do so unanimously.*

In mid-January 1964, I saw Tai again in order to resolve some obscurities concerning the old land case, and we decided to drive to the formerly disputed area. On the way I asked him about a recent meeting of the KANU leaders, and he was again evasive. After nearly a year in Embuland I felt rather secure and decided to gamble: I asked why KANU was not allowing me into its dispute settlement meetings. Clearly uncomfortable, Tai made several partial replies: that KANU really had no dispute settlement meetings; that I was asking him to tell me everything; and that KANU proceedings were secret, and he could not tell me about these. Further along the road were two other KANU leaders going our way. I picked them up and, after customary greetings, told them my earlier question to Tai which, I said, he had refused to answer. Tai asked my interpreter to stop translating because he wanted to talk to one of the leaders: They discussed something unrelated to politics. Shortly thereafter we dropped the other leaders. Tai and I were together for another hour or so, but the previous question was not raised again.

That evening I felt that I might have damaged my relationship with the party by forcing the issue, but in fact the situation continued to improve slowly.

One of the leaders whom we had given a ride was my fictive mother's niece. As she left the car she pointed to me the way to her house and suggested that I come to her feast for KANU women next Sunday. This was in line with a couple of very cordial gestures she had made during the previous couple of months. During the next six weeks I became slightly more daring. I told two other leaders that I had come to Embu to understand the nature of Embu society. They knew that I had spent hundreds of hours talking with old men about the precolonial society: I had learned about the important ancient institutions, the descent groups, age sets, generation sets, and so forth; but I was also interested in the contemporary society: the administration, the churches, the cooperatives, and the political party. If the leaders refused to tell me about their work, how was I going to understand this important part of the contemporary society? These leaders replied that *they* didn't suspect me any more, but many people remembered the Mau Mau days and were hostile to all foreigners.

From previous experience I knew that these leaders could tell me about their work only at the risk of severe disapproval from their colleagues, and there was no reason at all why they should choose to incur this disapproval. My general standing with the party could improve substantially only if the leaders approved of me unanimously. So I told the friendly leaders that I thought there was one particular old leader, Ngare, who continued to be hostile to me. They agreed with this and also with a proposal that I explain to Ngare directly what I was doing.

I knew that Ngare had long led his descent group in land litigation, was a member of the Co-op Managing Committee, and owned a sawmill. So I visited him one afternoon and explained my interests in Embu society, mentioned his many leadership roles, and my long-standing desire to talk with him. However, I had felt that he didn't want to talk with me; since I would shortly leave the field, I had come to see him and answer any questions he might have about me and my work.

Ngare said that he didn't want to ask any questions: God had given each his work, and he wasn't questioning people about theirs. We chatted cordially about the Co-op briefly; then Ngare said that he was sorry he had nothing to tell me: His heart told him not to talk with me. I replied that I agreed with him in that one should not do anything against the feelings in one's heart. The interview was over.

While Ngare had unquestionably slammed the KANU doors in my face, his colleagues continued to help me in small nonpolitical ways; their goodwill could not be doubted. This was two months after Kenya's independence. The government was now placing sharp limits on the number of political rallies, and the party activity seemed to decline considerably. I was in Embu for nearly six more months. I concentrated on other matters, learning only bits of political information here and there.[4]

Concerning my rapport difficulties with KANU, it is appropriate to raise several questions. Why was the party cold toward me in the beginning? Why did

---

[4] Saberwal (1969) presents the results of this research, blended wih documentary and other sorts of data.

some of its leaders begin to trust me more later? Was their increased trust justified?

While it is true that non-Africans were generally suspect in the eyes of most Embu at this time, it is likely that the mode of my initial introduction to Embuland prejudiced my case in the minds of KANU leaders. My initial contacts had been with the government officials in Nairobi, with the Provincial Commissioner's Office, the District Commissioner's Office, the District Officer, and then the chief and the subchief. It was still, then, a colonial administration, though being rapidly Africanized on the way to independence. By and large, the local party leaders perceived the administration as an adversary, and I had come to Embuland through the enemy camp. One might ask whether my prospects would have improved had I gone to Embuland through the party and not the administration. Quite apart from the fact that the administration controlled important resources such as houses, furniture, government records, and the like, it should be remembered that the administration constituted a salaried, reliable hierarchy, the juniors routinely trusting and accepting instructions from their seniors and acting upon them. The party apparatus, in contrast, was made up of volunteers, often dedicated men and women, whose range of competence and coordination was yet limited. They did deliver massive voter support for the party candidates at elections, but it would be an unduly optimistic view to assume that, for example, old man Ngare would have taken any advice from Nairobi as to my trustworthiness. In other words the ability of the political party in Kenya, 1963, to introduce the anthropologist into an area for general nonpolitical enquiry was much less than that of the administration; furthermore, the locational party was autonomous enough to ignore any directives from above. Thus, during the elections in May 1963 the KANU candidate was opposed by an Independent: the two men belonged to different parts of Embu Division, and each had the full support of the KANU organization near their home areas. Consequently, in a poll of over 28,000 persons, the official party candidate won by less than 900 votes. The discipline exercised by the party over its local units was loose, at best, in the Kenya of 1963, though the situation could be different at other times and places.

Beginning with an unfavorable image in the party minds, then, I was limited to observing the contexts defined by the party to be public. This fitted in well with my general practice of multiple, simultaneous projects. After about a year of fairly sustained attempts at channel building, it was clear that several party leaders were trusting me increasingly. My previous account has suggested that the leaders' trust in me grew in response to a series of smart moves by me; this may be entirely wrong. The reasons for their trust may well lie in what I did not do rather than what I did do, though they did not discuss this matter with me.

In the early months of my fieldwork, informants had often expressed fears that I had come there to "investigate" them. During the previous decade the Embu had learned to fear the numerous investigations characteristic of the Mau Mau Emergency; the objective of these investigations was to determine the subject's loyalty to the government, and those found wanting in this quality had invariably been punished. This investigation had often been secret, done without the subject's knowledge. Although the KANU leaders knew that I was curious about them, I think they also found out that I was not "investigating" them regarding their personal qualities. Now this was fortuitous: I had no ethical compunctions about inquiring about x from y if x happened to be relevant but hostile to my work. Had a political leader been living in my block, and had he refused to do the census with me, I would probably have tried to get the relevant information from a kinsman or neighbor; quite likely, this would have been interpreted as the dreaded "investigation" and might have brought me into some difficulties. However, in the party, my interest was in the structure of political activity and of decision-making, the recruitment process, and the strategy for winning an election; individual actors in this situation were interesting but not really important. So as the leaders gained assurance that I was not "investigating" in the sense that had dominated their previous experience, and as the evidence of my goodwill mounted, they decided that I was worthy of their trust—but was I?

The question can be answered in the affirmative, but only partially and tentatively. As far as I know, no one has yet used my data or analyses to harm the Embu or the peoples of Kenya generally. Once I publish my work, however, I have no control over who uses the information and to what purposes; that it may be used by some group within or outside Kenya to exploit the Embu is part of the existential anxiety I have to endure (Beer 1949). That the covert agencies of the United States government use social science information (and the social scientists) in their extensive operations abroad has been documented too often to need reiteration (for example, Langer 1967, or Nelson 1966, or van den Berghe 1967).

There is, besides, a more serious charge confronting anthropologists, which we have yet to answer. With our eyes set firmly on professional advancement in North America, nearly all of us report our findings in professional journals and in monographs addressed to other anthropologists (and their students), concentrated in overwhelming numbers in North America and western Europe. A few copies of these trickle through to other countries, but the poor countries (where most of us do research) rarely have the foreign exchange to import enough books, even those concerning their own lands. When we synthesize the literature and publish surveys, whether for the undergraduate or the lay reader, again the audience in mind almost invariably is North American and west European. Thus, social scientists who do field research abroad increase the informational resources of their home countries in relation to the areas where they do fieldwork. Information is the ultimate support for power, and thus we help the rich countries become more powerful in relation to poor countries. That the United States foundations and governmental agencies should contribute generously to this endeavor is understandable; why the citizens of poor countries should be asked to submit to this new form of exploitation and source of domination is less clear.

5

An Inward Focus:
A Consideration
of Psychological Stress
in Fieldwork

RONALD M. WINTROB

The success of fieldwork is largely the result of the unique interaction between the personality of the fieldworker, the nature of the research problem, and the general socio-cultural environment in which research is undertaken (Frances Henry).

The primary purpose of this chapter is to illustrate the nature of psychological stress reactions of anthropologists undertaking fieldwork. The descriptive accounts are drawn from the personal experiences of a group of graduate students with whom I met for a series of seminars aimed at the clarification of psychological problems inherent in fieldwork.[1] I have also drawn on autobiographical reports of other fieldworkers which illustrate some of their emotional reactions. The emphasis is placed on the reactions of individuals who have not had extensive fieldwork experience. A secondary purpose of this chapter is to consider some points of comparison between the personality structure of the "eminent" anthropologists studied by Roe (1952, 1960) and the graduate students who participated in the discussion group mentioned.

The literature on psychological stress reactions of fieldworkers is by no means extensive, although one is frequently told that such data exists in the personal field notes of many anthropologists.[2] Rosalie Wax is one of the few anthropologists who have published their personal reactions to the experience of

---

[1] Minor modifications have been made in the accounts of the students' experiences in some cases in order to protect the identity of individual students.

[2] Apparently most anthropologists are very sensitive about those experiences, preferring to keep their data well hidden from the scrutiny of colleagues and students (and from themselves, perhaps).

fieldwork (Wax 1960b). She points out that she did so reluctantly after repeated urging from colleagues "distressed by the scarcity of detailed accounts of how an investigator works" (Wax 1960b:166).[3]

Psychological stress of fieldwork covers a wide range, but certain categories of stress do emerge. For purposes of description these categories may be identified as: "maintaining the image," "the bias of personality," and "the dysadaptation syndrome." The "dysadaptation syndrome" may be further divided into what may be conceptualized as "conflict of involvement," "conflict of commitment," and "conflict of return."[4] These topics are discussed here in sequence.

When a graduate student undertakes his first independent fieldwork, his role identity—his image of himself as competent and knowledgeable in his field —is very much at stake. Rosalie Wax describes it as a sink-or-swim experience.

> In the past young anthropologists often embarked on a first field trip in a spirit not unlike that of adolescent primitives facing initiation into the tribe. In solitary agony, supported only by the wise sayings of their anthropological ancestors, they met their crucial and mysterious ordeal (Wax, 1960a:90).

In his paper "The Ethnologist as Stranger," Nash writes:

> A career and a reputation may hinge on the ethnologist's brief participation in the life of one of these ["primitive"] societies. In making the jump from a civilized to a primitive situation, in establishing rapport, and in attempting to acquire fairly complete data on the culture in a few months, the ethnologist encounters an extreme condition of strangership which lends a "do or die" atmosphere to his expedition. For few other strangers is the adaptive problem so extreme, and for few does so much hinge on successful adaptation (Nash, 1963:157).

Berreman (1962) laments the dearth of information on "the practical problems" of carrying out fieldwork, such that

> the person facing fieldwork for the first time . . . may suspect ethnographers of having established a conspiracy of silence on these matters. . . . As a result of the rules of the game which kept others from communicating their experience to him, he may feel that his own difficulties of morale and rapport . . . were unique and perhaps signs of weakness or incompetence. Consequently, these are concealed or minimized (1962:4).

This is one part of the psychological burden the relatively inexperienced fieldworker sets out with. Another part is comprised of repeated admonitions about

---

[3] A striking feature of her analysis of this period of fieldwork as a graduate student is the fact that Wax describes herself in the third person: "The anxiety which this student suffered in trying to defend the self of which she approved was so agonizing that she was unable to describe it adequately in her document" (Wax 1960b:175). It would appear that even in writing up the material, Wax may have wanted, consciously or otherwise, to increase her emotional distance from the "agonizing" experiences. The need to maintain an emotional distance may be a factor too in "fictionalizing" the description of an emotionally difficult period of fieldwork, as Bowen has done in her fascinating book *Return to Laughter* (1954).

[4] These categories are adapted in part from the analysis of psychological stress reactions of Peace Corps volunteers reported by English and Colmen (1967).

the bias of personality. In *The Foundations of Social Anthropology* Nadel considers the validity of the fieldworker's data in the light of his personal psychodynamics. He contends that

> Where the data observed are . . . human data, the observer's personality might easily override the best intentions of objectivity. In the final interpretation of the data some such bias is probably inevitable. . . . He cannot but . . . unconsciously respond to a context emotionally weighted with the emotional side of his nature (1953:48, 49).

In an attempt to come to grips with this issue, Bennett worked out a training course that would encourage students to realize that "the good field worker must work with and through his 'biases,' become aware of them, control them and use them" (1960:431). He feels that the student who "sees that *awareness* of these 'biases' is essential" [1960:436] may be "led to a 'realistic' concern with the anxious side of life in a closed society" (1960:439). Support for Bennett's position is found in Williams' account of his experiences with the Dusun of North Borneo. He states that

> human beings in every culture rationalize, project and sublimate their desires, wishes and fears. . . . [The Dusun] avoided talking about aggression while being highly aggressive, openly boasted of sexual conquests while actually being conservative in sex activities. . . . We found that one way of determining the accuracy of Dusun cultural data was the identification of the ego-defense processes widely shared and used in that culture (1967:27).

Bearing in mind then the stresses with which the fieldworker sets out on his research, how are these stresses reflected in the difficulties of adaptation he encounters in the field? For, as Nash points out, "How well or ill he adapts to the condition of his field role may determine what he sees, how he thinks, and therefore the nature of his report on the people he has studied" (1963:149–150).

The Dysadaptation Syndrome

Conflict of Involvement

Initial experiences may play a large part in determining the degree and ease of the fieldworker's involvement in the life of the community he has come to study. This is well illustrated by the experiences of one of the graduate students participating in the seminar, whose first fieldwork assignment was to determine the social structure of an urban minority group. His first interview with a key informant turned out to be easygoing and very productive. On the crest of his elation over the success of this test as a fieldworker, he went on to another key informant and was shocked by the brusqueness with which his attempts to obtain information were refused:

> He said he was just too busy, that I could come back next month and he might be able to talk to me: "We've had these students like you down here before

doing social studies. If you're interested, go see the priest." He implied I could go back and talk to him later on, but I never did. I just dropped it more or less. There were intervals for two or three weeks that I wasn't there at all. I kind of got discouraged going down there and knowing that you can't get anywhere beyond the first few opening remarks.

One can see that his self-image as an adequately trained social scientist was badly shaken by his uncooperative informant lumping him in with students doing "social studies." His reaction was to withdraw.

However, withdrawal may not be easy or even possible. One of the graduate students doing summer research on drinking patterns among Indians living in a northern town, and whose work required that contacts be maintained with both Indian and white communities, described the situation as follows: "You just couldn't be alone. No matter where you went you had someone asking you how your research was going, saying to come here and there, or this and that might interest you. And if you refused you could easily cut yourself off."

Describing her initial emotional reactions to living for a winter with a nomadic Eskimo family as the adoptive daughter of the Utku hunter Inuttiag, Jean Briggs gives this poignant account. "I was afraid in those first weeks: afraid of freezing to death, of going hungry, of being seriously ill and unable to reach help. The fear itself added to my chill, causing me to curse futilely at my own anxiety" (1968:320). She goes on: "mishaps seemed to occur constantly, and the smallest one assumed momentous proportions in my imagination" (1958:322).

Withdrawal, emotional if not physical, was one way Briggs tried to cope with her anxiety. When she was awakened to give tea leaves to her adoptive mother, "I seethed inwardly at the disturbance. . . . To me sleep is sacred. I cherish it, and in those days it was even more precious than usual, protecting me as it did . . . from the vicissitudes of the day . . . [and,] above all, [from] the necessity to hold myself in check" (1968:331). She could also withdraw into her tent, and she experienced intense feelings of helplessness which turned into panic when her "father" decided that she should abandon her own tent and move into the family *qaqmaq.* "My tent had become a refuge, into which I withdrew every evening . . . to repair ravages to my spirit with the help of bannock and peanut butter. So reviving were those hours of self-indulgence that I dreaded their loss" (1968:333).

Here Briggs touches on her second means of trying to cope with her stressful situation. In the face of extreme isolation from familiar social and intellectual sources of emotional satisfaction, where her security was completely in the hands of someone she hardly knew and had strongly ambivalent feelings about, an intensification of dependency needs was inevitable. Since it was essential that she not openly express her frustration and anger toward her "father," she attempted to relieve her insecurity by eating.

Rosalie Wax reacted very similarly to the stress of living at a relocation center for Japanese-Americans suspected of disloyalty during World War II (Wax, 1960b). During the first few months there her motives were highly suspect by the Japanese-Americans whom she had come to study. They thought, not surprisingly, that she had been sent by the United States government to spy on them. In this initially hostile environment Wax reports, "At the conclusion of the first month of work I had obtained very little data, and I was discouraged, bewildered and obsessed by a sense of failure" (1960b:168). In her analysis of these feelings twelve years later, Wax says that she was intensely anxious, trying to maintain and defend to her own satisfaction her role identity as "observer of sociological phenomena." Unable to maintain this role identity because of her own misconceptions of what it might entail, and faced with hostile informants, "She spent days alternately crying or writing letters to relatives and academic friends. . . . Finally she succumbed to an urge to eat enormously and in three months gained thirty pounds" (1960b:175).

Wax has alluded to another means of coping with the hostile impulses generated by the frustration of being dependent on informants who are guarded and suspicious, if not openly hostile. The fieldworker finds himself writing letters of a length and intensity of feeling that is not at all characteristic of him. Or the fieldworker finds that he is spending most of his time dictating into his tape recorder and typing it up in field notes. He seems to have no free time to carry out interviews or make contacts with potential informants. This experience was common to all the students during their initial period of fieldwork.

Wax also points to the motivations underlying these responses. "If a trusted person had asked her whether she was doing good work, she would have admitted that she was not. But she dared not admit it to herself" (1960b:176). Wax, like the students familiar to me, seems to have counted so heavily on the emotional gratification she anticipated from being recognized as a skilled ethnologist that she could not abandon some of the images and expectations she had identified with that role and her performance of it.

During the early period of fieldwork, anxiety that builds up tends to be free floating. It relates to environmental stresses, health concerns, and self-image, with fears of rejection by the community, feelings of inadequacy in collecting essential data, and fears of failure in completing the planned research. This type of free-floating anxiety was described by a graduate student who had spent the summer in a community of subarctic region Algonkian Indians.

> I was afraid of everything at the beginning. It was just fear, of imposing on people, of trying to maintain a completely different role than anyone else around you. You hem and haw before making a leap into the situation. You want to retreat for another day. I'd keep thinking: am I going to be rejected? Am I really getting the data I need? I knew I had to set up my tent but I'd put it off. I'd put off getting started in telling people about wanting to give a questionnaire. I was neatly ensconced in ———'s compound (an area of tents comprising one kin group). Everybody there knew what I was doing. I found it hard to move over to the other camp (a few miles away). I rationalized that a field worker shouldn't jump around too much.

However, free-floating anxiety must become focused to be contained. This need to focus anxiety is particularly strong in an environment where the free expression of hostility represents a profound threat to social controls and is consequently negatively sanctioned. Hostility cannot be completely repressed, but it can be displaced. The common experience among fieldworkers of focusing frustration on their housing reflects just such (unconscious) displacement. The student referred to in the preceding paragraph illustrates this mechanism of defense against intolerable anxiety.

> I wasn't getting the data I would have liked, and I started to feel that if only I wasn't so uncomfortable in that bloody tent I'd feel more like working. One of the first nights after I got my tent up there was a gale. It was like living in a thunderclap and the damn dogs kept coming around, howling and trying to break into the tent.

The unaccustomed extent of the fieldworker's dependence and helplessness intensifies his hostility. Briggs has touched directly on the intensity of simultaneous conflicting feelings over the many privileged services she received from her adoptive parents: "gratitude that I was taken care of and irritation that I was thereby placed under obligation" (1968:349).[5]

The next line of defense is projection of hostility; the unconscious attribution to another person of one's own feelings: "Inuttiaq announced in ringing tones: 'The tent is ruined!' So tense was the atmosphere at that moment that I was sure he had hacked the tent to pieces with his knife." As she repaired her tent Briggs "still mentally accused Inuttiaq of feeling satisfaction at the damage to my tent" (1968:377): One could paraphrase Briggs' feeling as: "You see, I am not angry at you, you are the hostile one. It is you who harbors malicious impulses toward me!"

The explanation of this phenomenon is simply stated by Nash: "The individual's inevitable frustration in all areas, including the perceptual, may cause him to blame the external world, particularly the hosts" (1963:154).

The physical and emotional dependence of the fieldworker on his key informants and "adoptive family" is at least matched, if not surpassed, by his dependence on his interpreter. This is one reason why the fieldworker devotes such special effort to selection of his interpreter.[6]

After some four months of attempting to establish rapport with suspicious and sometimes hostile villagers in India, Berreman had begun to feel that concerted research efforts could be fruitfully undertaken when his interpreter became ill and had to leave the region. "This was a disheartening blow. It plunged my morale to its lowest ebb in the fifteen months of my stay in India, none of which could be described as exhilarating" (1962:9).

The student I have described who withdrew from further contact with the urban minority group he planned to study following a sharp rejection by a key informant was bitter about not having an "in" in the community, but he eventually found one.

---

[5] However, hostility cannot be completely repressed or neutralized by displacement. Sometimes it reaches the surface. When Inuttiaq once asked her directly if she was angry at him, Briggs recalls, "I blushed and hesitated, gesturing 'no' and 'yes' simultaneously" (1968:379).

[6] Buechler describes this in some detail in an earlier chapter, as does Berreman (1962) in *Behind Many Masks.*

> The biggest break came when I got to know this woman who told me what was going on and introduced me to people. We went together to the places she knew. She was so well liked that you didn't have to watch all the small things you do and say. She worked there, *but she also thought a lot about what went on.*

The psychological importance to the student of this "buffer personality" is obvious, but I would stress too the important rationalization of his dependency needs. Faced with feelings of hopeless, angry futility over his initial failures, he assigns to this buffer personality the role of associate investigator. She effectively collects the data for him.

The ease with which the fieldworker develops rapport is largely determined by the role image he creates in the minds of his informants and the community as a whole. The conceptual divergence between the fieldworker's image of his role and that held by the community he is studying may be considerable. Williams refers to this divergence as false status-role assignment. He points out that the fieldworker may be variously regarded as a government informer, tax agent, policeman, missionary, or incarnation of ancester spirit or deity (1967:43–44).

This source of stress and the response to it is illustrated by one of the seminar graduate students.

> I was surprised how well the Indians took me in at first. But after a while they stopped taking me in. They stopped talking to me. At the time I saw it as a process of their accepting me at the beginning because I might be useful to them. But I wasn't very useful really. Then I got hints I was possibly a spy for the government Fish and Game Department. I became afraid to do too much after that. I was afraid I might say something wrong. I spent an awful lot of time alone when I knew [what they suspected because of] the threat of being ignored or made to feel uncomfortable if I tried to talk to people.

When he did interview someone, the long silent periods characteristic of Indian social interaction made him exceedingly anxious. "I suppose that when I'd get that feeling in the pit of my stomach I'd withdraw even more. I'd arrange to go hunting or chopping wood with some Indians and try to get information that way."[7]

One false status-role assignment not specifically discussed by Williams is the role of healer. It is a common experience among fieldworkers that they find themselves distributing a variety of medications commonly used in their own culture, but viewed with considerable awe in cultures in which such drugs, or any form of effective medical treatment, are nonexistent or in very short supply.[8] Describing his efforts to establish rapport in a Himalayan village, Berremen re-

---

[7] This is a case of sublimation of hostile impulses. His frustration with the Indians for making his personal adjustment and research task so difficult is channeled into the socially useful activities of hunting and chopping wood. He represses his hostile impulses toward the Indians and rationalizes his activity on the grounds that he will have a good opportunity to collect important data.

[8] It must be recognized that the distribution of medication may be interpreted by the shaman, native healer, diviner, or herbalist as a serious threat to his status in the community and accordingly may be widely resented. It may also be interpreted as evidence that the fieldworker may be attempting to "witch" people by giving them these unfamiliar medicines.

marks that: "We won some good will by providing a few simple remedies for common village ailments" (1962:9). The impact of providing these "everyday remedies" may be much greater than the fieldworker realizes. This may have been the case with Williams, who was accompanied by his wife, an experienced nurse, during his fieldwork with the Dusun. "We were asked for first aid in childbirth, burns, amputations, major cuts from fights, and fractures; for help in treating epidemics; and to alleviate pain from terminal cancers. My wife had clinics twice daily and we made it known we would come to give aid in the village" (1967:16). When the time came to leave the village a year later, Williams notes that: "We had to convince at least two older neighbours they could live on without our personal administration of vitamins and aspirin. Several mothers came to us extremely worried about the health of their infants" (1967:56). In just this way the fieldworker become identified as a crucial participant in the life of the community, and to many, an omnipotent medicine man. In view of this, it comes as no surprise when Williams remarks that "we have become aware from letters that our time of residence in Sensuron is marked now as 'the year the white woman lived here' and that babies delivered by us are named for us" (1967:58–59).

The reports of the group of graduate students suggest that this role may be unconsciously encouraged by relatively inexperienced fieldworkers as a means of self-validation. Their need for emotional gratification is intensified by threats to their self-image such as I have described. The greater their frustration, the more intense becomes their need for alternate forms of emotional gratification. In this manner, some of the students proceeded from distributing pills for headache to transporting the more seriously ill to hospital, and from that to acting as an increasingly vital intermediary between the hospital and the community. As the demands on his services increase, his ability to cope effectively with the growing expectations of his skills and competence decreases, and in several cases a high degree of anxiety was generated.

Conflict of Commitment

As the fieldworker struggles through some of his conflicts of involvement in the sociocultural milieu he has come to study, as he establishes working relationships with interpreter and key informants and rapport within the community, so he gradually comes to identify with his informants and the community as a whole. The feeling of responsibility toward the community grows partly out of a sense of relief that the fieldworker's most profound anxieties about his health and safety, and then about his adequacy and competency as an ethnologist, have not materialized. He feels rather ashamed of the groundlessness of his fears and guilty about the extent of his anger toward the community and his inability to effectively control its expression. It is partly out of an underlying need for expiation—to redeem himself in the eyes of his informants—that some relatively inexperienced fieldworkers drift into an overdetermined role as healer or other authority figure.

In other cases the degree of social distance separating fieldworker and informants may become so indistinct that the fieldworker becomes anxious about maintaining objectivity and becoming more of a participant in events than an observer of them.[9]

One of the graduate students did research on delinquent behavior patterns of a group of young adults of a cultural minority. There was little age difference between the student and his informants. He found, to his surprise and relief, that his efforts to penetrate the group met with little resistance or overt resentment. He began to go out with one of the girls in the group. The data seemed to roll in automatically.

> I got a fantastic amount of data. I was accepted by them. I was comfortable. About this time, though, I got extremely sick and my dependency on them increased a lot; they'd cook for me and keep me company. After that they just treated me as one of the group. They expected me to hang around with them all the time. They'd take me with them when they'd go on a "job." They stole for kicks, but usually they'd only steal from people they thought had money to replace the things, or from a company. I guess I sympathized a little, really. It was kind of funny.

As his emotional involvement with the girl and with the group itself increased, however, this student's relief and gratification in collecting rich and complete data with so little effort became transformed into anxiety. He became aware of being "sucked in" himself, began to wonder if he was being "used" by the group for its own amusement. How could he break his relationship with the girl without offending the group? He ultimately became dimly aware of the deeper psychological issues implicit in his study; to what extent were his reactions being motivated by his own needs for group belonging, and for the vicarious acting out of his own rebellious impulses?

This particular example illustrates a conflict common to all the students at this stage of fieldwork; the conflict over reciprocity. The students became acutely sensitive to the possibility that they were "using" their informants, exploiting their generosity and friendship for the purpose of gathering data they needed to write their reports or prepare their dissertations. They felt acutely troubled by this "one-sided" relationship, and as they became more closely identified with the group they were studying, their desire to reciprocate kindness intensified. Here lies part of the explanation for continuing the role of healer, with its attendant satisfactions and risks. Here too lies the explanation for what a number of students recognized as a strong tendency to perform an expanding variety of services as intermediary or "culture broker" between "their" community and the surrounding or dominant culture of the region. These services would involve writing letters to relatives, procuring and transporting supplies and equipment, explaining the community's needs to government agencies, or acting as middleman in arranging employment. Again, the consequence of performing such "favors" was often the increasing expectations and increasing demands on the part of some members of the group. To an experienced fieldworker this situation presented problems, but was not threat-

---

[9] Henry touches on this problem in describing her research among the "elites" of Trinidadian politics and trade unions.

ening to his role-image.[10] To a less experienced fieldworker, however, this situation could, and often did, provoke a recurrence of the cycle of frustration, anger, and self-doubt that resulted in acute anxiety. The gnawing feeling at this point that he is being asked to do things beyond his means and beyond his control comes as a particularly hard blow to the student's self-esteem. He may begin to ruminate about who is exploiting whom. Another period of angry, depressed withdrawal occurred in several cases.

Another consequence of growing identification with and feeling of responsibility toward informants relates to what information the fieldworker should include in the report he will prepare. A conflict may arise between the wish to report the material in depth and the equally strong wish to avoid unfavorable judgments. He will not want to reveal information that may prejudice the favorable view his informants have of him, or to prejudice their security in their community or the larger society.

This is exemplified by the experience of the student investigating delinquency.

> They knew I was studying delinquency. And they knew they were stealing. I told them I was studying what some young people do and how it's different from what a society wants them to do. They knew I was collecting police statistics; they'd make a joke of it. But I don't think they really knew that I would use the information I got from them—the information about them—as the basis for my whole report!

This student felt caught in a web of commitments of his own unknowing construction. He was in marked conflict over opposing impulses, on the one hand, responsibility and a deep wish to protect the group from trouble with the police, on the other hand, the wish to write a detailed, insightful account of the activities of the group. "I became aware that my own part in the relationship I had with them wasn't exactly honorable."

Conflict of Return

The dysadaptation stresses associated with this phase begin with the fieldworker's feelings about leaving the field, loosening the affective ties to interpreter, informants, and other individuals and subgroups in the community he has been studying. The stresses of separation are followed by those of reidentification of the fieldworker within his own culture and social milieu on his return from the field. This process bears closely on the degree and quality of the fieldworker's identification with the group he studied, and is reflected in the selection, interpretation, and

---

[10] In discussing role relations with informants, Williams points out that although he was expected to reciprocate when gifts of food or utensils were offered him, he was sometimes asked for "gifts of considerable value. We always attempted in these instances to find the reasons for such a request. . . . A mother of a baby near death from tuberculosis was desperately trying to raise the cost of a traditional curing ritual, while an old warrior wanted a trip in the airplane he saw flying over each week. In most instances we tried to arrange for the gift through securing the goods desired or by giving some equivalent" (1967:48–49).

write-up of the data he has collected. The relationship between the fieldworker's feelings of responsibility, his wish to benefit the group studied, and the nature of his research report is illustrated by the deep concern of the student about what he could and should report about the activities of the group of delinquents. Another seminar student put it this way: "Those people felt it was important for them to help [me]. They were pleased that someone was really interested in their lives, in their problems. And I saw my own responsibility in those terms; that my final report would help them!"

The student may recognize a strong desire to satisfy more than one group, or at least not offend them unnecessarily. This desire may generate marked anxiety when the groups are in conflict with one another. The student investigating drinking patterns among Indians was acutely sensitive of the implications of the Indians being branded as alcoholics on the strength of his report. He was afraid that the larger community would take his remarks out of context and extrapolate from them to satisfy its own hostile impulses toward the Indians and justify its prejudicial treatment of them. He was afraid that he might be deceiving or even betraying his Indian informants. He felt that people on all sides were expecting a great deal of him: the Indians, the local judiciary, municipal officials and police, the newspapers, and, finally, the research foundation and university which were supporting his work. He felt that all these people expected him not simply to provide information but to provide solutions to "the drinking problems" in the region as well. "I felt that I was being put under tremendous pressure; that everyone wanted me to confirm their own ideas. It took me about six weeks to write the first page [of my report]."

The fieldworker's identification with the group he has studied is a well-known phenomenon among anthropologists. In Nadel's words: "To each his field, explored by him, means an intensely personal adventure, almost a personal possession" (1963:51). Nash describes the situation more dramatically.

> Now, having undergone his ordeal by fire, he returns identified with a specific primitive tribe. Like people in other societies after a rite of passage the ethnologist has a new self after his field experience. Considering his emotional investment in this new self and the probability that "distance will lend enchantment" it may be that the return home reinforces both his alienation from the home society and the romantic pluralism which we have noted in the anthropological community (1963:164).

Personality Structure of the Fieldworker

> The role system of academic science seems to recruit and to depend on individuals who have largely rebelled against parental authority, who work as "lone wolves," who value intellectual over financial achievements. (Yehudi Cohen)

To what extent is this summary statement by Cohen of the work of Ann Roe (1961:223) applicable to the graduate students described in this chapter? In 1952 Roe reported on the psychological characteristics of a group of eminent social scientists, biologists, and physical scientists from whom she obtained detailed life history statements supplemented by Rorschach and TAT data (Roe, 1952, 1961).[11] There were eight anthropologists in the group. Most of them were from well-to-do families and tended to be the firstborn. Childhood illness (such as rheumatic fever or asthma) or constitutional problems (such as being overweight, underweight, or undersize) were prominent features in the lives of five of the eight anthropologists. They showed an early concern with the social status of the family and with interpersonal relations. They tended to be independent thinkers and high achievers with a lively interest in, but a certain detachment from, people.

In comparison with these eminent anthropologists, the majority of the group of seven graduate students did not derive from the upper-status social backgrounds, but did tend to be the firstborn. Childhood illness or constitutional problems played an important part in the lives of three of the students. For the majority, an early interest in interpersonal relations was associated with a generally lonely, solitary childhood.

The most striking similarities, however, are found in the areas of rebellion against parental authority and the struggle for a highly valued independence. Roe points out that "patterns involving overprotection and firm, if not overt, control are very common in the group" of social scientists (1961:215). They are "often troubled with conflicts over dominance and authority" (1952:25). Physical scientists and biologists do not show "anything like the extent of rebelliousness and family difficulty" characteristic of social scientists (1961:215). The TAT evidence suggests that "social scientists show many dependent attitudes and much rebelliousness, accompanied frequently by guilt feelings" (1961:216). The Rorschach responses demonstrate that "fairly free aggression . . . is clearer and stronger among anthropologists" (1961:218). Analysis of Rorschach materials suggests "a need to repress too direct an interest in persons" (1961:218). Roe relates the choice of a research career to the "basic importance of the need to achieve or to keep independence" (1961:220). She feels that social scientists' early concern with interpersonal relations is "related to their difficulties in freeing themselves from their parents" (1961:221).

The personal histories of the graduate students closely conform with Roe's findings outlined here. In several cases the career choice of anthropologist is itself a manifestation of rebellion against parental dominance, since it is strongly opposed and negatively valued by the parents. For some students the selection of their subject of research may represent, at a level very close to conscious awareness, an attempt to cope with their own problems, to arrive at a better understanding of themselves. This was clearly the case for the student who did research on a socially deviant minority group, and for another student investigating a fiercely independent and marginal subgroup. Several students recognized in their desire to study a very remote society a sublimation of the wish to proclaim their independence and to validate the self-image they aspired to.

The struggle for independence, for self-understanding, for validation of the individual's identity is a normal process in adolescence and early adulthood (Erikson 1959). It is only natural, therefore, that graduate students in their twenties

---

[11] A most interesting discussion of Roe's findings is provided by Nash (1963).

should give evidence of conflict in these areas. The intensity of the conflict is, nonetheless, very striking. Examples appear in profusion in the life history data. One student, for instance, after describing a particularly conflictive childhood of frequent arguments with parents and fights with siblings in which "I was always lying and stealing and getting into trouble," went on to recount a recurrent day-dream of "the perfect life." The scene is an island; "I'm dependent on no-one. I get everything from nature." This student wants to do fieldwork in a society relatively untouched by acculturative changes.

Another student gave this account of his research: "I think in this study I was looking for kicks—odd characters—marginal. It's marginality itself that interests me. I don't know why." His parents were perplexed by his career choice and moderately opposed, but his relationship with them had never been close. Childhood illness and constitutional problems had restricted his activities and caused him to withdraw from competitive interaction with peers. He was painfully shy and preoccupied with rather esoteric intellectual activities in childhood and adolescence. Adolescent rebellion and exploratory activity were very prominent in this case.

Talking about parental attitudes, another student said:

I leave the house every day at eight in the morning and I don't get back until one in the morning. I don't think I can live the way my parents want me to, but they're not giving me the freedom to decide. At times I honestly hate them for the way they want me to live; "come home early, don't make friends with anyone who isn't ———— [a member of the student's ethnic group]. My friends' parents are the same way, but this does not bother them as much.

Speaking about the coming summer of fieldwork in a remote area, and the career choice of anthropology, this student remarked that "the whole idea filled *them* with fear, but they still think they can change me back into a lawyer or an accountant."

A final example pertains to the high achievement motivation of the social scientist as described by Roe. Here, the student's father, a factory supervisor, is described as

authoritarian and domineering, quick to fly off the handle. And he's selfish; like pushing me through school. It was always, "excel, excel, excel," because it enhanced his own position. All through high school and university I stood first, won this, won that. He's very eager for me to get my Ph.D. because it will be like his getting a Ph.D. too.

Needless to say this student was very ambivalent about completing doctoral requirements.

From the examples I have quoted, one might contend that the only thing they illustrate is normal adolescent turmoil. However, it is also possible that the clarity and intensity of the conflicts over independence and rebellion against parental authority are reflected in the career choice of anthropologist, and the definite preference shown by these students for academic work and field research. In my view, the similarity in these specific aspects of personality structure of the group of graduate students with the personality structure of the eminent social scientists studied by Roe is far from coincidental.

I would like to conclude this chapter with a question. If it is true that psychological stress reactions are as common and as important to the performance and reporting of field research as this report would suggest, then what practical means could be utilized to extend the fieldworker's understanding of his own psychological needs and responses, and to broaden his understanding of the psychological significance of the reactions of the people he sets out to study?

References

ALMOND, G. A., AND S. VERBA, 1965, *The Civic Culture*. Boston: Little, Brown.

BEALS, R. L., 1967, Problems of Anthropological Research and Ethics. *Fellow Newsletter, American Anthropological Association* 8:1.

BEER, SAMUEL H., 1949, *The City of Reason*. Cambridge, Mass.: Harvard University Press.

BENNETT, JOHN W., 1960, Individual Perspective in Field Work. In *Human Organization Research*. Richard N. Adams and Jack J. Preiss (eds.). Homewood, Ill.: The Dorsey Press, 431–440.

BERREMAN, GERALD D., 1962, *Behind Many Masks*. Society for Applied Anthropology, Monograph No. 4, Ithaca, N.Y.

BÉTEILLE, ANDRÉ, 1965, *Caste, Class and Power*. Berkeley: University of California Press.

BONILLA, F., 1964, "Survey Techniques." In *Studying Politics Abroad*, R. E. Ward (ed.). Boston: Little, Brown, 134–152.

BOWEN, E. S., 1954, *Return to Laughter*. New York: Harper & Row.

BRIGGS, JEAN, 1968, Utkuhiksalingmuit Eskimo Emotional Expression: The Patterning of Affection and Hostility. Doctoral dissertation. Cambridge, Mass.: Harvard University Press (in press).

CASAGRANDE, J. B., ed., 1960, *In the Company of Man*. New York: Harper & Row.

COLSON, E., 1967, Competence and Incompetence in the Context of Independence. *Current Anthropology* 8:92–100, 109–111.

DIAMOND, S., 1964, Nigerian Discovery: The Politics of Field Work. In *Reflections on Community Studies*, A. J. Vidich, J. Bensham, and M. R. Stein (eds.). New York: Wiley, 119–154.

ENGLISH, JOSEPH T., AND JOSEPH G. COLMEN, 1967, Psychological Adjustment Patterns of Peace Corps Volunteers. In manuscript, 1–11.

ERIKSON, ERIK H., 1959, *Identity and the Life Cycle*. Psychological Issues, Monograph 1. New York: International University Press.

EVANS-PRITCHARD, E. E., 1940, *The Nuer*. New York: Oxford University Press.

GLUCKMAN, M., 1961, Anthropological Problems Arising from the African Industrial Revolution. In *Social Change in Modern Africa*, A. W. Southall (ed.). New York: Oxford University Press, 67–82.

———, ed., 1964, *Closed Systems and Open Minds: The Limits of Naivety in Social Anthropology*. Chicago: Aldine.

GOUGH, K., 1968, Dissent in Anthropology. In *Dissent in Social Science*, T. Roszak (ed.). New York: Pantheon.

GUTKIND, P. C. W., 1962, The African Urban Milieu: A Force in Rapid Change. *Civilisations* 12:167–195.

———, 1967a, Comment on Colson. *Current Anthropology* 8:105–106.

———, 1967b, Orientation and Research Methods in African Urban Studies. In *Anthropologists in the Field*, D. G. Jongmans and P. C. W. Gutkind (eds.). Assen: Van Gorcum, 133–169.

GUTKIND, P. C. W., JONGMANS, D. G., JONKER, C., KÖBBEN, A. J. F., SANKOFF, G. and SERPENTI, L. M., 1967c, Annotated Bibliography on Anthropological Field Work Methods. In *Anthropologists in the Field*, D. G. Jongmans and P. C. W. Gutkind (eds.). Assen: Van Gorcum, 217–227.

HENRY, F., 1966, "The Role of the Fieldworker in an Explosive Political Situation." *Current Anthropology* 7:552–559.

JONGMANS, D. G., AND P. C. W. Gutkind, eds., 1967, *Anthropologists in the Field*. Assen: Van Gorcum.

LANGER, ELINOR, 1967, Foreign Research: CIA plus Camelot Equals Troubles for U.S. Scholars. *Science* 156:1583–1584.

LEACH, E. P., 1967, An Anthropologist's Reflections on a Social Survey. In *Anthropologists in the Field*, D. G. Jongmans and P. C. W. Gutkind (eds.). Assen: Van Gorcum, 75–89.

LE GROS CLARK, F., 1953, The Conditions of Technical Progress. In *The New West Africa: Problems of Independence*, B. Davidson and A. Ademola (eds.). London: Allen and Unwin, 141–168.

LÉVI-STRAUSS, C., 1966, Anthropology: Its Achievements and Future. *Current Anthropology* 7:124–127.

MALINOWSKI, B., 1967, *A Diary in the Strict Sense of the Term*. New York: Harcourt.

MAQUET, J. J., 1964, Objectivity in Anthropology. *Current Anthropology* 5:47–55.

MITCHELL, R. E., 1965, Survey Materials Collected in the Developing Countries: Sampling, Measurement and Interviewing Obstacles and Intra- and International Comparisons. *International Social Science Journal* 17:665–685.

NADEL, S. F., 1953, *The Foundations of Social Anthropology*. New York: Free Press.

NASH, DENNISON, 1963, The Ethnologist as Stranger: An Essay in the Sociology of Knowledge. *Southwestern Journal of Anthropology* 19:149–167.

NELSON, BRYCE, 1966, Anthropologists' Debate: Concern over Future of Foreign Research. *Science* 154:1525–1527.

POWDERMAKER, H., 1966, *Stranger and Friend: The Way of an Anthropologist*. New York: Norton.

RALIS, M., E. SUCHMAN, AND R. K. GOLDEN, 1958, Applicability of Survey Techniques in Northern India. *Public Opinion Quarterly* 22:245–250.

READ, K. E., 1965, *The High Valley*. New York: Scribner.

RICHARDS, A. I., 1961, Anthropology on the Scrapheap? *Journal of African Administration* 13:3–10.

ROE, ANN, 1952, A Psychological Study of Eminent Psychologists and Anthropologists, and a Comparison with Biological and Physical Scientists. *Psychological Monographs* 67:1–55.

———, 1961, A Psychological Study of Eminent Psychologists and Anthropologists, and a Comparison with Biological and Physical Scientists. In *Social Structure and Personality*, Yehudi Cohen (ed.). New York: Holt, Rinehart and Winston, Inc., 212–223.

SABERWAL, SATISH, 1968, Political Change among the Embu, 1900–1964. In *East African Micropolitics*, Aidan Southall (ed.). (In press.).

SPECKMANN, J. D., 1967, Social Surveys in Non-Western States. In *Anthropologists in the Field*, D. G. Jongmans and P. C. W. Gutkind (eds.). Assen: Van Gorcum, 56–74.

SOUTHALL, A. W., AND P. C. W. GUTKIND, 1957, *Townsmen in the Making: Kampala and Its Suburbs*. East African Studies No. 9. Kampala: East African Institute of Social Research.

VAN DEN BERGHE, PIERRE L., 1967, The CIA and the Warfare State. *Transition* 33:75.

WAX, ROSALIE H., 1960a, Reciprocity in Field Work. In *Human Organization Research*, Richard N. Adams and Jack J. Preiss (eds.). Homewood, Ill.: The Dorsey Press, 90–98.

———, 1960b, Twelve Years Later: An Analysis of Field Experience. In *Human Organization Research*, Richard N. Adams and Jack J. Preiss (eds.). Homewood, Illinois: Dorsey Press, 166–178.

WILLIAMS, T. R., 1967, *Field Methods in the Study of Culture.* New York: Holt, Rinehart and Winston, Inc.

WILSON, E. C., 1958, Problems of Survey Research in Modernizing Areas. *Public Opinion Quarterly* 22:230–234.